Hebrews
FINDING THE BETTER WAY

Hebrews
FINDING THE BETTER WAY

Ron Phillips
FOREWORD BY R.T. KENDALL

Pathway
PRESS

Book Editor: Wanda Griffith
Editorial Assistant: Tammy Hatfield
Copy Editors: Esther Metaxas
Oreeda Burnette
Cresta Shawver
Inside Layout: Mark Shuler

Library of Congress Catalog Card Number:
ISBN: 0-87148-422-6
Copyright © 2001 by Pathway Press
Cleveland, Tennessee 37311
All Rights Reserved
Printed in the United States of America

DEDICATION

I dedicate this volume to

Dr. James McClanahan,

the executive pastor of Central Baptist Church.
I am thankful for all that Jim does
to allow me the time to study, pray, write and preach.
It is Jim's love of expository preaching
that has encouraged me to release these sermons in book form.

Contents

Acknowledgments

I am grateful to *Dan Boling* (general director) and *Bill George* (editor in chief) of Pathway Press for their strong encouragement and dedication to this project.

Also, I gratefully acknowledge the media staff at Central Baptist Church for their excellent work updating the manuscript. A special thank-you to Margy Barber for her careful editing of the manuscript. Also, thanks to Angie and Doug for the title and cover; their creativity undergirds my ministry.

Foreword

With a style that is both profound and readable, Dr. Ron Phillips offers a fresh approach to the Epistle to the Hebrews. His message is easily applicable, and would lend itself well to the spoken word. Throughout this book, Dr. Phillips conveys an awesome respect for the power and effectuality of the inspired Word of God.

Upon our introduction, Dr. Phillips and I formed an instant connection. Perhaps this can be explained by the fact that over the years, he and I have fought similar battles. Dr. Phillips and I are aware of the desperate need for the remarriage of the Word and the Spirit, and have both been the brunt of attacks from those who don't grasp this need.

It is evident in the church that there has been a division, in terms of emphasis and experience, between the Word and the Spirit. The simultaneous delivery of the Word (through expository preaching and sound doctrine) and the Spirit (through gifts and miracles) is possibly the most urgent need of the church at the present time. Ron Phillips seeks to meet this need through his preaching and writing, and this focus elucidates the rapid growth and influence of his church in Hixson, Tennessee.

It is my prayer God will use this book to inspire ministers and laity to seek a fuller understanding of the Word and experience total immersion in the Holy Spirit. In times that are sadly characterized by a form of godliness but a denial of its power, this book should cross denominational lines and usher in the mighty awakening we desperately need today.

Even as it was a privilege to read this life-changing book, it is my honor to recommend to you Dr. Ron Phillips' *Hebrews: Finding the Better Way.*

—R.T. Kendall
Westminster Chapel, London

Preface

The plans and purposes of God are never at a stand-still; our God is always marching on! When Christians or churches become satisfied with simply "holding their own," they are actually losing ground. To live on past glories means to forfeit future blessing.

The Christian life, from the new birth of salvation to the New Jerusalem of our heavenly home, ought to be a record of progress and growth. Unfortunately many Christians have never moved beyond spiritual infancy and immaturity. The Book of Hebrews speaks to Christians, encouraging them in spiritual growth, and calling out to the church of today, "Do not retreat, but march forward in faith!"

Our present generation needs the message of Hebrews. Churches have been slowly strangling on the ropes of tradition and ritual. Individual Christians often remain in spiritual kindergarten when they should have long ago graduated to live the adventure of faith.

Hebrews *exalts the Savior* to His proper place as sovereign over all the church. When Christ reigns as Lord over the church, the church will grow and progress like never before. Furthermore, Hebrews *exhorts the saints* to run the race of life with eyes firmly fixed on Jesus. Let this study encourage you to rise up and run the race until you see Jesus, the author and finisher of our faith!

Introduction

The Human Penman

Much debate surrounds the possible authorship of the Letter to the Hebrews. The apostle Paul has traditionally been regarded as its author, but many other names have been suggested. Even early church leaders were divided over the issue.

Clement of Alexandria (A.D. 153) held the view that Paul actually wrote it in Hebrew and Luke translated it into Greek.

Origen (A.D. 185) suggested Luke wrote the book.

Tertullian (A.D. 155) believed Barnabas penned the letter to the Hebrews.

Martin Luther (1483) favored Apollos as the author.

Adolf von Harnack (1851) felt that Aquila and Priscilla authored the letter.

Sir William Ramsay (1852) believed Philip was the author.

Scholars have called into question the authorship of a number of New Testament books, including 2 Peter, Revelation, all of the Gospels, and many other books. Sadly, solid facts are often overlooked for the sake of a good argument. Though a good number of scholars reject Pauline authorship of Hebrews, many of the objections can easily be answered.

At the end of the second century, Clement of Alexandria addressed the first of these objections, namely, the supposed inconsistent vocabulary and absent signature of the author. He believed Paul wrote it to

Jewish Christians in the Hebrew language, and, as mentioned, Luke then "diligently translated it into Greek." Fourth-century theologian Eusebius felt that Paul purposely did not mention his own name in the opening because he was the apostle to the Gentiles, while the Lord himself was the apostle to the Jews.

The question of vocabulary can be answered if you accept Clement's suggestion of the original text being written in Hebrew, and understand that Paul was a scholar of the first order and could adjust his style to his audience.

Some question Pauline authorship because they feel Hebrews presents a different view of Old Testament law than Paul held. However, this restricts Paul to only one approach to the Old Testament and questions the unity of Scripture as a whole.

Some also say Paul couldn't have written Hebrews because he never before emphasized the priesthood of Jesus like it is presented in this letter. However, that is not so. Paul clearly taught the mediatorial work of Christ and His heavenly session at the right hand of God.

Another objection is that Paul had a different view of faith than the view presented in Hebrews (as if the Bible presented more than one view). How can anyone read Hebrews 10:22 and deny the connection with Paul? "Let us draw near with a true heart in full assurance of faith, having our hearts sprinkled from an evil conscience, and our bodies washed with pure water" (KJV).

Is it possible that 2 Peter 3:15, 16 is a reference to the Epistle to the Hebrews?

"And consider that the longsuffering of our Lord is salvation—as also our beloved brother Paul, according to the wisdom given to him, has written to you, as also in all his epistles, speaking in them of these things, in which are some things hard to understand, which untaught and unstable people twist to their own destruction, as they do also the rest of the Scriptures."

In addition, Hebrews 13:23 gives us another clue to Pauline authorship because it mentions Timothy, who was the companion of Paul: "Know that our brother Timothy has been set free, with whom I shall see you if he comes shortly."

Finally, though Paul was the apostle to the Gentiles, he still had a great burden for the Jewish people. Paul would especially have grieved over Hebrew Christians forsaking their new faith and the church to return to Judaism.

The Purpose

Most commentators agree that the recipients of this letter were Jewish Christians who were being drawn back into Judaism from their newfound faith in Jesus Christ.

The letter has a distinctively Jewish flavor. It contains numerous references to Old Testament Scriptures. Much of the letter is concerned with seeing Christ as the great fulfillment of Jewish ritual and the sacrificial system. Throughout Hebrews, Jesus is declared to be both High

Priest and Sacrifice. He is shown to be superior to, as well as a fulfillment of, the Old Testament. Hebrews 11 also gazes back to Old Testament times with its summary of Old Testament acts of faith.

Why was there a need for such a letter to Jewish Christians? To understand the situation of these believers, you must imagine what it must have been like for these early Christians who left the Temple, the synagogue, and all the rituals of Judaism. Their lives had been built around these rituals. The great holy days were the key events of their lives. And yet, they left this secure life behind when they embraced Christ. Very often when they left Judaism, parents and family would actually have a funeral for the new convert, effectively banishing the believer from the home. What terrible discouragement this must have been for these believers!

Furthermore, there is evidence in Hebrews that these believers were being persecuted in other ways. We find that Hebrews seeks to remind them of the temptation and testing of Christ and encourages them to remember that He would come to their aid in trials (2:18; 4:14-16). Hebrews 10:32, 33 clearly speaks of intense persecution.

These Jewish believers were wavering in faith and their spiritual growth had been stunted. They were still serving, but they were "sluggish" (Hebrews 6:12).

The Plan
This book is an exhortation meant to encourage some very discouraged, defeated and disappointed

saints. Look at these passages: Hebrews 3:13; 10:25; 12:5, 6; 13:19, 22. The author is encouraging the saints in their lives, telling them that although they are tired and weary, someone is alongside the race-course cheering them on. The Letter to the Hebrews is a strong word of encouragement. These Jewish Christians longed for the comfort of their past lives and feared the uncertainty brought by persecution. Some were ready to give up. This was written to cheer them onward.

Several words are keys to understanding this letter. One word is *better.* It is found throughout the letter. Jesus is seen as "better than the angels" (1:4) and providing a "better hope" (7:19), "a better covenant" (7:22), "better promises" (8:6), "better sacrifices" (9:23), and "better blood" (12:24, paraphrase). This emphasizes the superiority of Jesus Christ.

THE PATTERN

An outline will help us see the author's plan and brings into focus the main divisions of the book.

Outline of Hebrews
Theme: The Supremacy of Jesus Christ

THE SUPREME WORD (1:1–4:13)
    An Ultimate Word (1:1–2:4)
        God has spoken finally! (1:1-3).
        God has spoken clearly! (1:4-14).
        God has spoken urgently! (2:1-4).

An Incarnate Word (2:5–3:6)
   Jesus' preeminence as a man (2:5-9)
   Jesus' passion as a man (2:10-16)
   Jesus' priesthood as a man (2:17–3:6)
An Accurate Word (3:7–4:13)
   Accurate in its inspiration (3:7)
   Accurate in its declaration (3:8–4:11)
   Accurate in its revelation (4:12, 13)

THE SUPREME WORK (4:14–10:18)
   Jesus' Work as Forerunner (4:14–6:20)
      His earthly work as our Help (4:14–6:8)
      His heavenly work as our Hope (6:9-20)
   Jesus' Work as Intercessor (7:1-28)
      Old Testament illustration (7:1-24)
      The order of Melchizedek is the oldest order of priests (7:1-10).
      The order of Melchizedek is now the only order of priests (7:11-24).
      New Testament application (7:25-28)
   Jesus' Work as Mediator (8:1–10:18)
      Mediator of a better covenant (8:1-13)
      Mediator of a blood covenant (9:1–10:18)

THE SUPREME WAY (10:19–13:21)
   The Invitation to Faith (10:19-39)
      We are to draw near (10:19-25).
      We are not to draw back (10:26-39).
   The Illustrations of Faith (11:1-40)
      The obtaining of faith (11:1-3)
      The offering of faith—Abel (11:4)
      The operation of faith—Enoch (11:5, 6)

The obligation of faith—Noah (11:7)
The obedience of faith—Abraham (11:8-10, 17-19)
The offspring of faith—Sarah (11:11, 12)
The observation of faith—the City (11:13-16)
The outcome of faith—Isaac, Jacob and Joseph (11:20-23)
The opportunity of faith—Moses (11:24-29)
The overcoming of faith—others (11:30-40)
The Inspiration of Faith (12:1-29)
The inspiration of the race (12:1-3)
The inspiration of the rod (12:4-17)
The inspiration of the reward (12:18-29)
The Influence of Faith (13:1-21)
Influence evident in how one loves (13:1-6)
Influence evident in how one lives (13:7-19)
Influence evident in how one labors (13:20, 21)

CONCLUSION (13:22-25)

PROBLEMS

Five passages in Hebrews have been considered problem passages by students of the Bible. Many believe that these passages teach the possibility of apostasy, or losing your salvation. The five passages, or warnings, are interspersed within the body of Hebrews.

Hebrews 2:1-4. This is the warning against the neglect of salvation. Author and teacher Dr. Warren Wiersbe speaks of it as an exhortation not to "drift from the Word," while scholar Dr. John Phillips calls it a warning not to "disregard salvation."

Hebrews 3:7–4:13. This is a warning against the hardened heart. It speaks to the peril of unbelief, the dangers of doubting or disbelieving God's sufficiency to save.

Hebrews 5:11–6:20. This passage speaks of apostasy. It is indeed the most difficult of the passages. Dr. Wiersbe calls it "dullness toward the Word." Dr. John Phillips says this warning has to do with "discrediting the Son of God."

Hebrews 10:26-39. This passage speaks about the danger of willful sin. Dr. Wiersbe says it is talking of a call not to "despise the Word." Dr. John Phillips says it has to do with "despising the Spirit of God."

Hebrews 12:15-29. In this passage, we find reference to a refusal or indifference to the Word, warning those who are disobeying the summons of God.

These passages will be studied in their respective contexts later in this book. I personally feel that they underline the utter seriousness of the matter of salvation and they hold up the truth that God is completely able to preserve the salvation of those who commit themselves to Him unreservedly.

THE PROMISE

It is my prayer that through your study of Hebrews, you will come to understand the hope and faith that is available when you choose the better road—one of complete dependence on Christ and dedication to uphold His cause no matter what the influences are around you. Let God's Word flood your soul and help you find the better way—the path of obedience that is the core of the faith life!

1

God's Last Word

*God, who at various times and in various ways spoke
in time past to the fathers by the prophets, has in these
last days spoken to us by His Son, whom He has
appointed heir of all things, through whom also He
made the worlds; who being the brightness of His glory
and the express image of His person, and upholding
all things by the word of His power, when He had by
Himself purged our sins, sat down at the right hand of
the Majesty on high. . .* (Hebrews 1:1-3).

INTRODUCTION

Hebrews does not begin with authorship or
argument. Rather, this glorious book begins with
a shattering announcement. The earth-shaking
declaration is that God has spoken a final word
to the world.

The audience that first heard this announcement was made up of Hebrew Christians who
were in danger of drifting from the reality of Christ
and drawing back into the rituals of Judaism.

God had spoken to them in the past. He spoke
at "sundry times and in diverse manners . . ." (1:1,

KJV). This speaks of the variety and fullness of the former revelation. God had spoken in the awesome thunders of Mount Sinai. He had whispered in a still, small voice to Elijah on Mount Horeb. God's glory was written in the majesty of the mountains and in the varieties of colorful life.

God spoke in the beautiful rhyming lyrics of the Psalms. His heart of love and tenderness is heard in the Song of Solomon. The prophets declare His righteous judgment in burning eloquence. You can almost hear His voice breaking along with His great heart in the tender Book of Hosea. The gospel is clearly foreshadowed in Isaiah. In Jeremiah, the hurt of rejection rings through His Word. In Ezekiel and Daniel, God's Word is heard in magnificent mystery.

From Moses to Malachi, over a period of more than 1,000 years, God's Word was witnessed, recorded and declared. Yet, standing in the wings of history was God's final message to man. God's last word to humanity rings out in the message of the angel to Mary, "You . . . shall call His name Jesus" (Luke 1:31). Also, it is heard in the message of the angels to the shepherds, "There is born to you this day . . . a Savior, who is Christ the Lord" (Luke 2:11, KJV).

Though Jesus stood in the wings of history waiting for His time, He cast a long shadow throughout the Old Testament. All of the books of the Old Testament, like tributaries into a mighty river, merge into the last word of God to man, Jesus. All of the shadows became substance in Him. All of the voices of the prophets merge together in one triumphant shout, "Glory to the Son of God!"

In the opening verses of Hebrews, we discover seven things said of Jesus that cannot be said of anyone else in history.

Jesus is the ruler of God's universe. An heir is one who receives an inheritance from another. The Lord Jesus Christ has received from the Father the title deed to all things. In Matthew 28:18, Jesus said, "All authority has been given to Me in heaven and on earth." In Philippians 2:9, 10, Jesus is given, "the name which is above every name, that at the name of Jesus every knee should bow, of those in heaven, and of those on earth, and of those under the earth."

No one can question His absolute sovereignty and dominion. As owner of all, He has a rightful claim on human lives. Revelation 11:15 speaks of that day when all the "kingdoms of this world have become the kingdoms of our Lord, and of His Christ."

Jesus is the reason for God's creation. The Lord Jesus Christ was the agent of creation. In general, we have a record of what God said; and what God the Father said, God the Son carried out. John 1:3 says, "All things were made through him." Colossians 1:16 says, "For by Him all things were created." The word *ages* reminds us that Jesus is Lord over creation and history. He not only created the material universe, he also ordered the very epochs of time. Jesus is the reason for creation.

Jesus is the radiance of God's glory. The glory of God is the manifestation of all His divine attributes— the shining forth of His glorious person. In the Old

Testament, the glory of God hovered as a shining cloud above the Holy of Holies. That glory rested on the ark of the covenant. When Jesus came, the glory of God came in person. What Moses did not fully see, all who know Jesus can experience. Moses asked to behold the face of God. God revealed the hind parts of His glory, but the joy of knowing His glory was reserved for those who found God after the Cross, for God revealed His full glory in Jesus Christ.

Jesus is the King of Glory. Psalm 24:7 says, "Lift up your heads, O you gates! And be lifted up, you everlasting doors! And the King of glory shall come in." God's glory touched earth when Jesus was born. When we have an encounter with Jesus, we are transformed into the same image from glory to glory.

Jesus is the revealer of God's character. The words "express image" (Hebrews 1:3) translate into the word *character* in the Greek. It is used to refer to an engraving that creates an exact impression or replica of something. Jesus Christ perfectly displays the character of Holy God. The Lord Jesus Christ set forth the holiness, love, justice, mercy and grace of God. There is no need to wonder what God is like, or who God is—we have seen God in Jesus Christ.

Jesus is the regent of God's power. The word *uphold* means "to bear a load." It speaks of support. It is the same word used in Mark 2 when the disciples carried the paralytic to Jesus. Jesus is the administrator of God's Word in the world. The word of Jesus is the word of power. What Jesus says, He has the dynamic power to sustain.

What a comfort for us to know that Jesus bears all the promises of God on the strength of His power. We are saved and kept by the word of His power. We are supplied by the word of His power. We are comforted, healed and helped by the power contained in the Word.

Jesus is the redeemer of God's people. Here we are introduced to Jesus, our High Priest who was sacrificed. He purged our sins, meaning that God has removed them completely and forever.

The Lord Jesus, unlike the Old Testament priests, offered Himself as our sacrifice. Furthermore, Jesus finished His work and then sat down. The Old Testament priests never sat down—they continually offered sacrifices. Our Lord Jesus cried from the cross, "It is finished!" and the sacrifice for sin was offered and accepted (John 19:30). Now our Lord sits at the right hand of the Father, indicating that His work is finished.

Jesus is the recipient of God's honor. Jesus did not stay in the grave. After receiving the deathblow of Calvary, He marched onto the battlements of death and hell, where He rendered helpless the forces of darkness and came out victorious and triumphant.

Jesus' march was not finished. He marched up through the clouds of the air, ascending through the galaxies and stars as they glorified Him. The angels of glory shouted their welcome as Christ marched to the throne. There at the Father's right hand, the place of honor awaited. The Father shouted across the ages as He saw His pierced Son, "This is My beloved Son, in whom I am well pleased!"

CONCLUSION

The Lord Jesus Christ has no rival or equal. He lays claim to your life. Today can be His coronation day in your heart.

2

King of Angels

Having become so much better than the angels, as He has by inheritance obtained a more excellent name than they. For to which of the angels did He ever say: "You are My Son, today I have begotten You"? And again: "I will be to Him a Father, and He shall be to Me a Son"? But when He again brings the first-born into the world, He says: "Let all the angels of God worship Him." And of the angels He says: "Who makes His angels spirits and His ministers a flame of fire." But to the Son He says: "Your throne, O God, is forever and ever; a scepter of righteousness is the scepter of Your kingdom. You have loved righteousness and hated lawlessness; therefore God, Your God, has anointed You with the oil of gladness more than Your companions." And: "You, Lord, in the beginning laid the foundation of the earth, and the heavens are the work of Your hands. They will perish, but You remain; and they will all grow old like a garment; like a cloak You will fold them up, and they will be changed. But You are the same, and Your years will not fail." But to which of the angels has He ever said: "Sit at My right hand, till I make

Your enemies Your footstool"? Are they not all minis-tering spirits sent forth to minister for those who will inherit salvation? (Hebrews 1:4-14).

INTRODUCTION

The Book of Hebrews does not name its human author. As stated in the Introduction of this book, through the ages scholars have had different opinions concerning the author of Hebrews.

I firmly believe Paul wrote this book in the Hebrew language and Luke translated it into Greek. Although Paul was the apostle to the Gentiles, as a Hebrew he still had a burden for the Jewish people. Hebrew Christians were reverting back to Judaism and Paul was concerned about them. They were drifting away from Christianity, and their spiritual progress was at a standstill.

Like many of us, these Christians were *listening* but not really *hearing* God's Word. All through the letter to the Hebrews, there is a call to *hear*. God had spoken, and Paul urged them to hear His voice and not "harden [the] heart" (3:8). The warning is clear: "See that you do not refuse Him . . . who speaks from heaven" (12:25).

Abundant Old Testament references are given to support the fact that God has spoken to the world through His Son. Jesus Christ is the supreme revelation of the Father. He is superior to all the Old Testament characters, including the hosts of angels.

Paul had a lot to say on the subject of angels. These heavenly beings are real; they exist to minister. They are invisible hosts who are servants of God. The Jews rightly believed that angels were the givers of the Law. Consider the following verses:

"Who have received the law by the direction of angels and have not kept it" (Acts 7:53).

What purpose then does the law serve? It was added because of transgressions, till the Seed should come to whom the promise was made; and it was appointed through angels by the hand of a mediator (Galatians 3:19).

In their reverence for the law, many Hebrew Christians had exalted the message of law above the message of grace given through Christ.

The angels are indeed glorious. They have acted and still act on behalf of God and Christians. Marie Monson, in her book, *A Present Help*, tells of her days in North China. Threatening bandits surrounded the compound where she lived. The compound was never penetrated, however, because the bandits believed they saw a band of bright soldiers. Marie Monson believes that heavenly hosts guarded the compound.

As glorious as angels are, they aren't equal to the Son of God. Seven Old Testament passages are quoted in Hebrews to emphasize the absolute superiority of Jesus above the angels. Paul chose these seven quotes no doubt to reveal Jesus' glory from His cradle to His crown.

THE TESTIMONY TO THE SON (1:4-6)

Three Old Testament quotes begin this section. The first two refer to Christ's first coming.

His Relationship as Son
(Hebrews 1:5; Psalm 2:7)

Jesus was already the eternal Son, but He came to earth in human form. In Luke 1:35, Mary was told that her Son would be called the Son of God. Again in Matthew 3:17, we learn more of His sonship as the Father declared, "This is My beloved Son." John the Baptist said of Him, "And I have seen and testified that this is the Son of God" (John 1:34). In Romans 1:4, we are told that Jesus is "declared to be the Son of God with power . . . by the resurrection from the dead."

His Royalty as Son
(Hebrews 1:5; Psalm 89:3, 4)

This is a reference to God's covenant to have a son of David on the throne. This Son was King of Israel. Second Samuel 7 records God's covenant with David, delivered to him by Nathan the prophet. The covenant included the following promises to David: the land of Israel to belong perpetually to the people of Israel (v. 10); David's house to be established and his successor to build the Temple (v. 13); and David's throne to be established forever (v. 16).

All these promises, God has kept, including the coming of Jesus, the Son of David, as King. Revelation 5:5

rightly describes Jesus as the "Root of David." He was both the root and offspring of David. He alone is the rightful King of Israel and of all creation.

His Return as Son
(Hebrews 1:6; Psalm 97:7)

Here we make reference to the second coming of Christ. In Jewish tradition, the firstborn inherited everything. When Jesus comes to claim His own and all the earth, the angels in heaven will bow in wonder and worship.

The name of Jesus is above any other name, including the angels. Michael is the glorious name of the angel of the Lord who watches over Israel. He is also the general of the Lord's hosts. Gabriel is the angel who served as messenger of the Lord, who carried the news of the Savior's birth to the world. But no angelic name can match the wondrous name of Jesus!

THE THRONE OF THE SON (1:7-9)

There are two quotes in this section of Scripture that further exalt our Lord Jesus Christ as superior to angels.

The Angels Stand Before the Throne
(Hebrews 1:7; Psalm 104:4)

Hebrews 1:7 indicates that the angels are servants who worship before the Lord. The word *seraphim* means "burning ones." I believe they are on fire to serve the Lord! They do not sit on the throne, but stand before it, ready to serve. This is clear by the angel's statement in Luke 1:19, "I am Gabriel, who stands in the presence of God."

The Son Sits Upon the Throne (Hebrews 1:8, 9; Psalm 45:6, 7)

Psalm 45 is a wedding psalm. It depicts the king, seated upon his throne, and the bride enthroned with him. These verses testify to the eternal nature of our Lord's reign.

You can sense in these words the reign of joy that takes place when Christ sits enthroned with His bride, the church. The word *gladness* in the original language implies "leaping with joy." The Lord Jesus, who was the Man of Sorrows, is now seen in great rejoicing over His bride.

THE TIMELESSNESS OF THE SON (HEBREWS 1:10-12; PSALM 102:25-27)

Psalm 102 affirms the eternal nature of the Son of God. Early in the chapter, we read of the rejection of Christ and His suffering, but the verses cited here declare His eternal and everlasting life!

The Lord is declared to be the Creator who will out-live His creation. Like a garment that is worn out, all of creation is degenerating. The Lord Jesus forever remains the same. He is eternal.

Again and again in Scripture, we discover that our eternal Savior has given us eternal salvation, redemption and an inheritance. Creation may change; angels may change; but Jesus is "the same yesterday, today, and forever" (Hebrews 13:8).

The Lord Jesus is always our contemporary. He is always relevant. This truth alone gives meaning to our lives. The eternal perspective keeps us from despair when the difficult times hit.

THE TRIUMPH OF THE SON
(HEBREWS 1:13, 14; PSALM 110:1)

This passage speaks of the victory of the Son of God. Psalm 110:1 is quoted, declaring that Jesus' work is finished, and now the Enemy will be brought under His feet.

The Lord Jesus is seated at God's right hand, a place of honor and authority. This is the second time in this chapter that the right hand of God is mentioned (Hebrews 1:3).

Our Lord quoted this psalm as He stood before the Pharisees and challenged them (Matthew 22:41-46). When He was on trial for His life, Jesus said to Caiaphas, "Hereafter you will see the Son of Man sitting at the right hand of the Power . . ." (Matthew 26:64). In Mark 16:19, we read, "So then, after the Lord had spoken to them, He was received up into heaven, and sat down at the right hand of God."

In the message of Pentecost, Simon Peter also quoted the same psalm, declaring Jesus to be exalted to the Father's right hand:

Therefore being exalted to the right hand of God, and having received from the Father the promise of the Holy Spirit, He poured out this which you now see and hear. For David did not ascend into the heavens, but he says himself: "The Lord said to my Lord, 'Sit at My right hand'" (Acts 2:33, 34).

Paul speaks of the right hand of God as the place where Jesus "makes intercession for us" (Romans 8:34).

Three more times in Hebrews, we are told that Jesus is at the right hand of God (8:1; 10:12; 12:2). What is the significance of that location? It is the place of victory! With Christ's work finished on the earth, He has now gone to glory where He awaits the final triumph. First Peter 3:22 declares of Jesus, " . . . Who has gone into heaven and is at the right hand of God, angels and authorities and powers having been made subject to Him."

Here, our triumphant Lord reigns in victory. He is Lord over the fallen angels. These forces have been defeated and are under His feet. He is Lord over the holy angels, who are servants of those He has delivered. These angels serve us, but they cannot save us. Their main job is to worship God and serve the saints of God. In Isaiah 6:3, the angels are found worshiping, crying, "Holy, holy, holy is the Lord of hosts." They served Isaiah in a ministry of discipline as they brought a coal from the altar to touch his unclean lips.

CONCLUSION

The only One who has the right to be worshiped

is the Lord Jesus Christ. He is King over the angels. Is He King of your heart? Will you believe the testimony of the ages? Will you come and bow before His throne of grace? Will you lay hold of the timeless One today? Oh, that we would learn to truly worship Him, coming into His presence to give Him all our honor and love!

3

The Tragedy of Neglect

Therefore we must give the more earnest heed to the things we have heard, lest we drift away. For if the word spoken through angels proved steadfast, and every transgression and disobedience received a just reward, how shall we escape if we neglect so great a salvation, which at the first began to be spoken by the Lord, and was confirmed to us by those who heard Him, God also bearing witness both with signs and wonders, with various miracles, and gifts of the Holy Spirit, according to His own will? (Hebrews 2:1-4).

INTRODUCTION

Dr. George Truett, former pastor of First Baptist Church in Dallas, once said, "Our whole world is a battlefield covered with wrecks occasioned by neglect."

Indeed, all of us have witnessed the ruin of some neglected building. Anyone visiting Nashville, Tennessee, would be able to tour The Hermitage, the beautifully kept mansion of former President Andrew Jackson. However, many years ago, I visited Andrew Jackson's other former home in Natchez, Mississippi, and was sad to see that old antebellum home in sad disrepair. Stepping on the porch of that neglected mansion, we had to kill a snake to proceed through the front door! Fortunately since then, that old home has been restored to its original beauty.

Sad instances of neglect abound in the miseries of human suffering. These extend from the nursing homes filled with sad seniors longing for a relative to stop by, to the little girl on a bus route early in my ministry who tugged on my coattail and asked, "Please mister, will you be my daddy?"

As sad as these pictures may be, the saddest and most tragic neglect in life is when someone rejects God's gift of salvation. Nearly as tragic is what Paul addresses in this chapter of Hebrews. The Hebrew Christians were not rejecting salvation, but were neglecting it. The same Greek word used for *neglect* in verse 3 is also found in Matthew 22:5, where it reads, "they made light of it." Basically, Paul was writing not to lost people, but to Christians who had begun to simply not care about their salvation.

THE REASON FOR NEGLECT (2:3, 4)

There are five warnings placed in Hebrews that are designed to remind people of the superiority of Christ. This first warning has to do with neglecting salvation.

People Don't Grasp Its Greatness

In this passage, the author boasts about "so great a salvation" (v. 3). Our salvation from God is unequalled and unparalleled.

Salvation is great because God designed it and gave it to man. "Which at the first began to be spoken by the Lord" (v. 3). God never does anything inferior. When God saved mankind, He provided a free, full, sufficient, universal and everlasting salvation.

The salvation purchased by the blood of Jesus has changed people through the centuries. Men have borne witness to the greatness of salvation since the early church. If we could call Simon Peter and Paul to the witness stand, they would testify to the power of this salvation. If great Christians could be called from all the ages of history, their witness would be, "It is a GREAT salvation!"

This great salvation was confirmed by "signs" witnessed by the Gentiles and by spiritual gifts to the church. You see, this great salvation is a powerful force. The gospel alone can break the shackles of sin and transform anyone into the image of Christ.

Its Uniqueness Is Forgotten

This passage asks the question "How shall we escape this salvation?" (v. 3). There is no escape! Christ's salvation is not the best way to heaven, it is the only way! Only one door, one way, one Savior, one fountain of living water exists, and that is Jesus Christ.

It is possible to be saved and neglect the provision of salvation, remaining in infancy and immaturity. The Book of Hebrews is a book of progress and growth, encouraging believers past the infancy stage into full maturity in Christ.

41

THE RESULTS OF NEGLECT (2:1, 2)

Neglecting salvation has a twofold result.

Danger of Drifting

The verse here reads, "lest at any time we should let them slip" (v. 1, KJV). The Greek word for "slip" is *pararrhueo*. The word can be used in many ways—one is that of a ring slipping from a finger and being lost. It is also used to refer to a jar that has a small, unnoticed crack that gradually leaks out all the contents. Another use refers to a vessel drifting on the water.

Indifference to Christ can bring heartache and loss of the spirit's power. My wife once lost her engagement ring, but that didn't mean she lost me! While the ring was precious to her, she had not lost the one who had given it to her.

A Christian can, like a leaky jar, lose the *fullness* of salvation. Gradually, we can become backslidden and lose the overflowing presence of the Lord. I remember the story of an old country preacher who seemed to be constantly preaching on the fullness of the Holy Spirit. One day a deacon asked him why he didn't choose another subject once in a while. The wise man of God replied, "Because you brethren all leak!"

Robert Robinson wrote the hymn "Come Thou Fount of Every Blessing," but later in his life, he became backslidden. One day, a fine Christian young lady who did not know him struck up a conversation with him. As they talked, she quoted a verse from his own song to him, and the words struck his heart, calling him to immediate repentance.

Prone to wander, Lord I feel it,
Prone to leave the God I love;
Here's my hear, O take and seal it,
Seal it for Thy courts above.

Too many Christians are a ship without an anchor or rudder, drifting aimlessly without stability or direction. This does not need to happen—Jesus can be both anchor to hold and rudder to guide us in the sea of life.

The great river of God's will is ever flowing on to bigger and more glorious purposes. Some individuals and churches are content to stand like children and splash in the shallow waters of complacency, while the greater plan of God for their lives flows right by.

Danger of Destruction (2:2)

This verse describes two kinds of sin. *Transgression* is the violation of God's standard. It is the word used for trespassing on someone else's property. It involves going beyond the boundaries established by God. *Disobedience* means failing to obey what God has told you to do. You could say that transgression is the sin you do; disobedience is the sin of not doing what you ought to do. God warns us that sin will bring judgment. If believers live in sin, they will be disciplined by Him. Lost people who die in sin will be eternally punished in hell.

THE REMEDY FOR NEGLECT (2:1)

I saved the first verse in this chapter for last because it holds the remedy for neglect. We are instructed to give

43

heed or apply our minds tenaciously, with total concentration, to the Word of God.

Dr. Warren Wiersbe is noted for his wonderful Bible studies and commentaries. He once told about a man in Leeds, England, who wore a hearing aid for years. Upon his visit to a new doctor, the physician removed the hearing aid and the man's hearing immediately improved! He had been wearing it in the wrong ear for 20 years!

Another pastor was asked if he had a deaf ministry in his church. He replied, "Sometimes I feel the whole church is deaf!" Christians should be the most attentive when it comes to the truth of the gospel. This quote by Dr. Griffith Thomas contains a dire warning: "With familiarity, truths tend to lose their influence, and the result is involuntary gradual backsliding."

Of course, it is possible to *listen,* but not truly *hear.* The Book of Hebrews is a call for Christians to commit to fully *hear* the message of truth. God wants our undivided attention.

CONCLUSION

I was in revival in Mississippi when a tragedy happened in the community. A man had accidentally backed his truck over his 4-year-old daughter, killing her. It was an accident, but one caused by neglect. At the funeral, it was heart-wrenching to watch the man's agony as he cried over the precious little life that was gone.

The man did not know Christ, and had rejected previous opportunities to accept salvation. After the funeral, the man cried to his pastor, "There could be no greater neglect than what I did to my child." The preacher responded, "No sir, you are wrong. Your own soul is in peril if you continue to run from the free gift of salvation Christ has offered to you."

Woe to the individual who neglects salvation, and to the Christian who takes the precious gift lightly. Let us be careful to praise Him continually for "so great a salvation" (Hebrews 1:3).

4
Death Destroyed—Life Restored

For He has not put the world to come, of which we speak, in subjection to angels. But one testified in a certain place, saying: "What is man that You are mindful of him, or the son of man that You take care of him? You have made him a little lower than the angels; You have crowned him with glory and honor, and set him over the works of Your hands. You have put all things in subjection under his feet." For in that He put all in subjection under him, He left nothing that is not put under him. But now we do not yet see all things put under him. But we see Jesus, who was made a little lower than the angels, for the suffering of death crowned with glory and honor, that He, by the grace of God, might taste death for everyone. For it was fitting for Him, for whom are all things and by whom are all things, in bringing many sons to glory, to make the captain of their salvation perfect through sufferings. For both He who sanctifies and those who are being sanctified are all of one, for which reason He is not ashamed to call them brethren, saying: "I will declare Your name to My brethren; in the midst of the assembly I will sing praise to You." And again: "I will put My trust in Him." And again: "Here am I and the children whom God has given Me." Inasmuch then as the children have partaken of flesh and blood, He Himself likewise shared in the same, that through death He might destroy him who had the power of death, that is, the devil, and release those who through fear of death were all their lifetime subject to bondage. For indeed He does not give aid to angels, but He does give aid to the seed of Abraham. Therefore, in all things He had to be made like His brethren, that He might be a merciful and faithful High Priest in things pertaining to God, to make propitiation for the sins of the people. For in that He Himself has suffered, being tempted, He is able to aid those who are tempted (Hebrews 2:5-18).

INTRODUCTION

When Jesus died upon the cross, great transfers of power took place in heaven, in hell and in the earth. By becoming human and dying, Jesus took on the limitations and temptations of humanity; yet through His death, mighty movements took place in the heavenly realms.

Hebrews 2:5-18 describes the purpose for the death of Jesus Christ. In verses 9 and 10, we read of His suffering, and how Jesus tasted death for us all. He was our substitute, taking upon Himself our suffering and drinking the bitter cup of death that we deserved.

In verses 14 and 15, we see Jesus as the victor over death. He has come to reverse the effects of Adam's fall. By dying for us, Jesus has given us four wonderful blessings.

He Restored Our Forfeited Inheritance (2:5-9)

The writer begins by quoting Psalm 8:4-6 in describing the supreme favor, special privilege and unique dignity of man.

"What is man that You are mindful of him, or the son of man that You take care of him? You have made him a little lower than the angels; You have crowned him with glory and honor, and set him over the works of Your hands. You have put all things in subjection under his feet" (vv. 6-8).

Man was also given complete domination over the earth, but forfeited that right when sin entered the scene. Man could not be the king of the earth as God intended, because instead of declaring God's glory, man abused the dignity and privilege given to him. Man lost his dignity; this can be seen in the moral and cultural climate of our world.

Humanity today is only a broken replica of what God intended us to be. You would not point to a demolished Rolls Royce and say, "Now that car is all it was intended to be." Neither can you point to man and say he has reached the heights of what God's purpose was for him.

Man was also crowned with glory and honor, but he forfeited that crown. However, by God's grace, Jesus came to restore what had been lost! As the Second Adam, the progenitor of a new humanity, Christ came and took a crown of thorns upon Himself, wearing it for us in the suffering of death. He was victorious over death and now wears a crown of glory and honor, which He has promised to all who trust Him.

He Has Reinstated Our Family Relationship (2:10-13)

When humanity fell into sin, something else precious was lost: a family relationship with God. Satan stole God's children and became their new father.

Jesus came to restore His children and holds the door open wide for all who trust Him to become a part of His family. His purpose as "captain of our salvation" is "bringing many sons to glory"(v. 10). As Captain, He is the pioneer, the trailblazer, the leader, and the author of our salvation. He has blazed the trail through the wilderness of our sin to bring us home to glory.

One of the themes of Hebrews is the idea that Jesus has come to bring us home (Hebrews 3:6; 11:10, 13-16). This world is not our final home; we are simply a part of God's vast new family who will eventually live with Him in glory.

Two Old Testament passages are cited to support this thought. They are Psalm 22:22 and Isaiah 8:17, 18. Psalm 22:22 states: "I will declare Your name to My brethren; in the midst of the assembly I will praise You."

After describing the death of Jesus, this psalm places Him in the midst of the church declaring the name of the Father and singing His praises.

Isaiah 8:17, 18 pictures God hiding His face from Jacob.

And I will wait on the Lord, who hides His face from the house of Jacob; and I will hope in Him. Here am I and the children whom the Lord has given me! We are for signs and wonders in Israel from the Lord of hosts, who dwells in Mount Zion.

The Father turned His face when Jesus hung on the cross. But Jesus' trust was in the Father, so we are made His children through His death.

Jesus is "not ashamed to call [us] brethren" (Hebrews 2:11). He is our brother and companion, and all that He has is ours. We are recipients of His love. All this is possible because He was willing to be a "perfect" Savior (v. 10). The word *perfect* here means "complete." Jesus was willing to do all that had to be done to give us complete salvation. He came to lead a new family home to glory.

Rick Stanley, now a Baptist minister, experienced the miracle of being pulled into a new family and a new home. As a young child, his father abandoned his mother. With no income, his mother had to put him and his brothers in an orphanage. However, Rick's mother remarried a man named Vernon Presley, and one day a fancy car came to pick up Rick and his brothers. The car drove right through the gates of Graceland, where he met his new stepbrother, Elvis Presley, who picked them up in his arms and said, "You're my brothers. . . you'll always be treated well here." The next morning they discovered a yard filled with toys, bicycles and gifts; they ran with joy from one item to another, amazed to find themselves in such a home.

That story is just a small picture of what Jesus has done for us. In the great song "A Child of the King," hymnist Harriet Buell rejoiced:

I once was an outcast stranger on earth,
A sinner by choice, an alien by birth,
But I've been adopted, my name's written down,
An heir to a mansion, a robe and a crown.

He Has Rendered Our Foe Powerless (2:14)

The death of Jesus was a death blow to Satan. The word *destroy* here means to "render inoperative or ineffective." The devil had the power of death. He did not have the authority to kill, but he had the might or the ability to kill. He was able to kill because "the wages of sin is death" (Romans 6:23). Sin was the only right that Satan could stand upon in order to kill. Satan's fatal mistake came when he endeavored to kill Jesus. It was the death of Jesus that removed Satan's right to kill sinful mankind. Jesus was innocent, and thus paid man's sin debt. Now Satan has no right to kill any child of God.

He Has Removed Our Fears Completely (2:15-18)

The Lord Jesus has taken away the greatest fears of humanity. First, the fear of death is gone forever. It is no longer the great unknown because He has charted a course through it. It is no longer a leap into the dark, because He has kindled the bright and morning star of the Resurrection. It is no longer a terrible sting, because He has taken the sting of death in His own body (1 Corinthians 15:51-56).

Second, Jesus has removed fear in the trials and testings of His people. He is our great merciful High Priest who reached out and reconciled us in spite of our sins. He is our mercy seat where we may come to cry for help.

He is our faithful High Priest in that when we call, He comes to help us. The word *succour* (Hebrews 2:18, KJV) really means "to run to help a crying child" (*boetheo* in Greek). In Matthew 15:25, the Syro-Phoenician woman cried out to Jesus, "Lord, help me!" The same word is used in this Hebrew passage. Christ is ready to come to our aid if we just cry out for help.

CONCLUSION

Through His death, Jesus has restored our inheritance, reinstated us into His family, rendered our foe powerless and removed our fears completely. Now He stands ready to come to our aid as He hears our cry. Won't you trust Him?

5
Where on Earth Does God Live?

Therefore, holy brethren, partakers of the heavenly calling, consider the Apostle and High Priest of our confession, Christ Jesus, who was faithful to Him who appointed Him, as Moses also was faithful in all His house. For this One has been counted worthy of more glory than Moses, inasmuch as He who built the house has more honor than the house. For every house is built by someone, but He who built all things is God. And Moses indeed was faithful in all His house as a servant, for a testimony of those things which would be spoken afterward, but Christ as a Son over His own house, whose house we are if we hold fast the confidence and the rejoicing of the hope firm to the end (Hebrews 3:1-6).

INTRODUCTION

This section deals with the house of God—the place God chooses to live on the earth. Across the years, God has chosen to live in at least six houses. Four of them were designed after the pattern given to Moses on Mount Sinai.

Along with Abraham, Moses was (and is) considered to be the central figure of Jewish history.

Moses is mentioned 70 times in the New Testament. He had divine protection and provision at his birth. He was called dramatically, through the miracle of a burning bush. He confronted the evil Pharaoh and led the nation of Israel through the Red Sea and to the border of the Promised Land. He faithfully received and delivered the Law and the pattern for God's first home on earth, the Tabernacle. Moses authored the first five books of the Bible and stands in Scripture as a man of faith.

As great as Moses was, the writer of Hebrews wanted to be certain the reader understood that Jesus is greater. Moses was God's servant; Jesus was God's only begotten Son. This unique passage contains interesting information concerning the habitation of God.

God's First House

We understand that God lived with Adam on the earth, but the first record of a dwelling built for God's habitation was the Tabernacle built in the wilderness by Moses. God gave him the pattern for this holy building on Mount Sinai. God gave the Law in the Ten Commandments, and gave grace in the Tabernacle and its sacrifices.

The Tabernacle had three sections—the outer court, the Holy Place and the Holy of Holies. The ark of the covenant, which contained the Law, was inside the Holy of Holies. The lid of the ark was called the mercy seat. This was God's throne on earth. Here, blood was sprinkled annually on the Day of Atonement. God's glory cloud, called the *Shekinah*, would hover above this place when God was there.

The same pattern and dimensions were used in building each of the temples erected by Solomon, Ezra and Herod. The Temple was God's house on Planet Earth. It was where He had chosen to dwell among man.

Exodus 40:34, 35 speaks of the glory of the Tabernacle: "Then the cloud covered the tabernacle of meeting, and the glory of the Lord filled the tabernacle. And Moses was not able to enter the tabernacle of meeting, because the cloud rested above it, and the glory of the Lord filled the tabernacle."

In 2 Chronicles 7:12, God spoke to Solomon. "Then the Lord appeared to Solomon by night, and said to him: 'I have heard your prayer, and have chosen this place for Myself as a house of sacrifice.'"

Haggai 1:8 declares that God was glorified in the rebuilt temple. " 'Go up to the mountains and bring wood and build the temple, that I may take pleasure in it and be glorified,' says the Lord." Jesus called Herod's temple, "My Father's house" (John 2:16).

Yet in every case, God moved out of these earthly houses. Perhaps the saddest picture in the Old Testament is the departure of the glory from Solomon's temple in the Book of Ezekiel. In the New Testament, Jesus expressed His grief concerning Herod's temple: "See! Your house is left to you desolate" (Matthew 23:38). Moses' tabernacle house was also glorious, but God moved out.

God's Faithful House

The Lord Jesus Christ called Himself a temple of God. "Jesus answered and said to them, 'Destroy this temple, and in three days I will raise it up.' Then the Jews said, 'It has taken forty-six years to build this temple, and will You raise it up in three days?' But He was speaking of the temple of His body" (John 2:19-21).

Surely it could be said of Christ as of no other that the glory of God dwelt on Him. He was born of a virgin and thus was not contaminated with the cursed blood of Adam. He was God living on the earth as He had never lived there before. However, the day came when Jesus became sin for us, and that house was desecrated. The Father moved out and Jesus cried, "My God, My God, why have you forsaken Me?" (Matthew 27:46). Jesus had said, "Destroy this temple, and in three days I will raise it up" (John 2:19). Jesus was superior to Moses, for while Moses built a tabernacle, Jesus was the Tabernacle!

God's Final House

"Whose house we are . . ." God now has a brand-new house in which to live. As Christians, we are now the household of God.

Now, therefore, you are no longer strangers and foreigners, but fellow citizens with the saints and members of the household of God, having been built on the foundation of the apostles and prophets, Jesus Christ Himself being the chief corner stone, in whom the whole building, being joined together, grows into a holy temple in the Lord, in whom you also are being built together for a dwelling place of God in the Spirit (Ephesians 2:19-22).

Paul tells us that we are God's building: "For we are God's fellow workers; you are God's field, you are God's building" (1 Corinthians 3:9).

He also said, "Do you not know that your body is the temple of the Holy Spirit who is in you? . . . " (6:19). Then he declares that the house of God is the church, the people of God (1 Timothy 3:15). Peter said, "Ye also, as lively stones, are built up a spiritual house" (1 Peter 2:5, KJV).

God has moved into a house to stay. He lives in the hearts of His people on earth! As His living house, we are a superior house to that of Moses' tabernacle. We are "partakers of the heavenly calling" (Hebrews 3:1). The word *partaker* is used elsewhere to describe our partnership with Christ in suffering (1 Peter 4:13), in His divine nature (2 Peter 1:4) and in His inheritance (Colossians 1:12).

Because we are His house, we are to make Him the object of our affection and attention. We are also to confess Him as Lord (Romans 10:9). Jesus said, "Therefore whoever confesses Me before men, him I will also confess before My Father who is in heaven. But whoever denies Me before men, him I will also deny before My Father who is in heaven" (Matthew 10:32, 33).

The end of this section of Hebrews tells us to "hold fast the confidence [in Him]" (v. 6). This phrase indicates keeping possession, seizing, keeping secure. In the Greek it is an aorist verb, and literally means "once for all." People become part of God's household if they have once and for all possessed, seized and secured faith in Christ.

We hold fast in confidence and boldness. This confidence will carry us to the end in joy.

CONCLUSION

God's preferred house is within our hearts. Ephesians 3:17 says, "That Christ may dwell in your hearts through faith." God wants to live in our lives. Your heart can be His house, but He will only come in by invitation.

6

Heart Trouble

Therefore, as the Holy Spirit says: "Today, if you will hear His voice, Do not harden your hearts as in the rebellion, in the day of trial in the wilderness, where your fathers tested Me, tried Me, and saw My works forty years. Therefore I was angry with that generation, and said, 'They always go astray in their heart, and they have not known My ways.' So I swore in My wrath, 'They shall not enter My rest.'" Beware, brethren, lest there be in any of you an evil heart of unbelief in departing from the living God; but exhort one another daily, while it is called "Today," lest any of you be hardened through the deceitfulness of sin. For we have become partakers of Christ if we hold the beginning of our confidence steadfast to the end, while it is said: "Today, if you will hear His voice, do not harden your hearts as in the rebellion." For who, having heard, rebelled? Indeed, was it not all who came out of Egypt, led by Moses? Now with whom was He angry forty years? Was it not with those who sinned, whose corpses fell in the wilderness? And to whom did He swear that they would not enter His rest, but to those who did not obey? So we see that they could not enter in because of unbelief.

Therefore, since a promise remains of entering His rest, let us fear lest any of you seem to have come short of it. For indeed the gospel was preached to us as well as to them; but the word which they heard did not profit them, not being mixed with faith in those who heard it. For we who have believed do enter that rest, as He has said: "So I swore in My wrath, 'They shall not enter My rest,'" although the works were finished from the foundation of the world. For He has spoken in a certain place of the seventh day in this way: "And God rested on the seventh day from all His works"; and again in this place: "They shall not enter My rest." Since therefore it remains that some must enter it, and those to whom it was first preached did not enter because of disobedience, again He designates a certain day, saying in David, "Today," after such a long time, as it has been said: "Today, if you will hear His voice, do not harden your hearts." For if Joshua had given them rest, then He would not afterward have spoken of another day. There remains therefore a rest for the people of God. For he who has entered His rest has himself also ceased from his works as God did from His. Let us therefore be diligent to enter that rest, lest anyone fall according to the same example of disobedience (Hebrews 3:7—4:11).

INTRODUCTION

One of the top 15 killer diseases in our day is arteriosclerosis, also known as hardening of the arteries. If left unchecked, it restricts blood flow and eventually causes the heart to stop. In recent years, great advances have been made in heart bypass operations to add years to the lives of those who suffer from the disease.

I fear that Christians live in danger of spiritual "hardening of the arteries." The writer of Hebrews expresses his concern about Christians becoming hardened and missing the blessings of salvation. This is the second of five warnings against drifting from the Word. Also included here is a warning against unbelief.

The Hebrews author draws this warning from Israel's history. Fearing the inhabitants of Canaan and disregarding the testimony of the brave spies Joshua and Caleb, who related the great blessings they spotted within the Promised Land, the children of Israel refused to move forward and take the land. They were thus condemned to wander 40 years in the wilderness when they could have entered their "land of milk and honey" through a simple 11-day journey! The writer of Hebrews quotes Psalm 95, written 1,000 years after that day of disobedience, to show that the lessons of history need to be heeded today. Israel hardened its heart against the word of God. Spiritual hardening set in, and the nation had to wait to enjoy their land.

The author of Hebrews was anxious for the Christians who seemed to make a good beginning to go on to possess all that was promised them. In citing the passage from Psalms, he affirms the Old Testament as the voice of the Holy Spirit of God. The first four chapters of the Book of Hebrews are concerned with the Word of God. God had spoken, and believers must not harden their hearts against His Word.

THE CAUSES OF A HARDENED HEART (3:7-13)
Delay (3:7-9)

The longer obedience is put off, the more danger-ous it becomes. Five times in this section of Hebrews, we find the word *today*. This seems to indicate the incredible grace that God extends to every period of history. It was "today" in Moses' day. It was "today" a thousand years later when David wrote Psalm 95. It is still "today." To delay in accepting His grace and dis-obey His word is to risk a hardened heart.

Restlessness (3:10, 11)

The Bible speaks of a straying and erring heart. Because the nation refused to follow the Lord with their whole hearts and strayed away from Him, God condemned them to stray for 40 more years without a home.

When you allow your heart and mind to stray into sin and disinterest, you face a danger of hardening. The great hymn "Come, Thou Fount of Every Blessing" records the prayer of hymn writer Robert Robinson:

Prone to wander, Lord, I feel it,
Prone to leave the God I love;
Here's my heart, O take and seal it,
Seal it for Thy courts above.

Unbelief (3:12)

God's Word has been spoken. To refuse to believe, time and again, is to risk a hardened heart. At that

64

point, believing will become difficult and even impossible, the mind clouded by doubt and despair.

Sin (3:13, 14)

Sin deceives, and will eventually cause the heart to harden. Ecclesiastes 8:11 says, "Because the sentence against an evil work is not executed speedily, therefore the heart of the sons of men is fully set in them to do evil." The more one sins, the easier it becomes, thus causing the heart and conscience to become numb to the prompting of the Holy Spirit.

THE CONSEQUENCE OF A HARDENED HEART (3:15—4:10)

Hebrews 3:18 states clearly, ". . . They would not enter His rest. . . " Ten times the word *rest* is mentioned in the passage. The main blessing missed by the disobedient children of Israel was *rest.*

What is rest? The Greek word means "to settle down." In classical Greek, it was used to speak of colonization of an area. Here we could believe it to mean to live "settled down with God," living totally dependent upon Him. *Rest* is a synonym for a life that is lived by faith; the antonym is *unbelief.*

Three examples of rest are discussed in this passage.

Israel's Rest (3:15-19)

The nation Israel refused to enter their promised land of plenty because of unbelief. When they finally entered, they further compromised their rest because they refused to drive out the enemies completely.

Father's Rest (4:4)

God finished His work of Creation and rested on the seventh day. What interrupted God's rest? Sin came in, and thus Jesus would say to the Pharisees, "My Father has been working until now, and I have been working" (John 5:17). I believe God started His work for our souls.

Jesus' Rest (4:10)

The Lord Jesus has now finished His work on the cross and has entered into His rest. All who put their faith in Him are invited to share in that rest.

Is your life unsettled? Are you at peace with God? Is your life an obedient life? Are you carrying your own burden? God wants you to have rest.

Our generation is marked by restlessness. We have more leisure, but no true rest. In Matthew 11:28-30, the secret of real rest is outlined:

- We must come to Jesus.

- We must receive His gift of rest.

- We must take His yoke.

- We must learn of Him.

We can have rest in our souls by resting in the future promise of eternal peace in heaven, as well as experiencing His comforting presence in the storms of this life on earth.

Don't miss out on the promised special blessing of the rest God gives. Hebrews 4:3 tells us that those who believe enter that rest. Let us learn to turn to His face to experience it.

THE CURE FOR THE HARDENED HEART

The cure is repeated throughout this passage in Hebrews. We must *hear* His word, listen to His voice (3:7). We should *believe* His word and mix it with faith so the result is profitable to our spiritual health (4:2). We should *obey* His word, going where He tells us and doing what He commands (4:11). Our Christian obligation is to *share* His word, encouraging one another (3:13). Coming alongside one another, we should seek to comfort and lift each other up until the day the Lord returns.

CONCLUSION

Jesus has delivered us from the slavery of sin. He desires to lead us into His rest, the place of total reliance on Him. Let us not become hardened against His Word, but go on into the Promised Land with Him. Though the Enemy may surround us, Jesus is alive and is our strong tower!

The story is told of a foreign missionary driving into a remote village who saw a native carrying a heavy load upon his head. The missionary stopped to give the native a ride on the back of his truck. The native tentatively accepted, approaching the vehicle with curiosity. After a while, the missionary looked back to see how the native was enjoying the ride and was surprised to see him standing in the back of the truck with the load still upon his head. When asked why he did not lay down his burden, the native replied that he was afraid the truck could not hold him and his burden too.

Let us not fear to lay our burdens down at His feet.
We need to learn that Jesus can carry any weight for us.

> They came to the gates of Canaan,
> But they never entered in.
> They came to the land of promise,
> But they perished in their sin.
> And so we are ever coming
> To the place where two ways part;
> One leads to the land of promise
> And one to a hardened heart.
> —Author Unknown

7

What Makes the Bible Different?

For the word of God is living and powerful, and sharper than any two-edged sword, piercing even to the division of soul and spirit, and of joints and marrow, and is a discerner of the thoughts and intents of the heart. And there is no creature hidden from His sight, but all things are naked and open to the eyes of Him to whom we must give account (Hebrews 4:12, 13).

INTRODUCTION

What makes the Bible different? The writer of Hebrews was concerned that believers see the importance of the Word of God. The supremacy of Scripture is emphasized again and again in the first four chapters. When God speaks, whether through the written Word or through Jesus, the living Word, it is different from the words of men.

Hebrews 4:12, 13 graphically describes the difference between His Word and all other words. All through this book, the believer is exhorted to give attention to the Word of God. What makes His Word different?

Different in Its Inspiration

The writer of Hebrews carefully describes that the Word has its origin in God himself. The immediate context contains a quote from the Old Testament. Though David wrote down Psalm 95, God spoke through this human penman. Hebrews 3:7 verifies this, for we are told that the Holy Spirit spoke Psalm 95. The entire Word of God is inspired—God-breathed. It is infallible and inerrant because an infallible God spoke it. It is verbally inspired, because every word came from the One who is Truth.

Different in Its Operation

The words of men can be flowery and effective in argument, but God's Word is living and powerful. Its operation is described two ways.

The Word is alive. The Greek word *zao* is used in this passage and is the same word from which we get our English word *zoology*. It means much more than just being "alive"; it has the meaning of "animate life." The Word of God is alive and gives life; it reproduces life in others.

The Word is active. The word *powerful* comes from the Greek word *energes*, from which we have gained our modern *energize*. The Word of God energizes and brings life where there is death. It brings activity where there has been inactivity.

The Bible stands in witness to itself. In Psalm 19:7-11, it converts the soul:

The law of the Lord is perfect, converting the soul; the testimony of the Lord is sure, making wise the simple; the statutes of the Lord are right, rejoicing the heart; the commandment of the Lord is pure, enlightening the eyes; the fear of the Lord is clean, enduring forever; the judgments of the Lord are true and righteous altogether. More to be desired are they than gold, yea, than much fine gold; sweeter also than honey and the honeycomb. Moreover by them Your servant is warned, and in keeping them there is great reward.

In Psalm 119:49-56, it encourages the heart:

Remember the word to Your servant, upon which You have caused me to hope. This is my comfort in my affliction, for Your word has given me life. The proud have me in great derision, yet I do not turn aside from Your law. I remembered Your judgments of old, O Lord, and have comforted myself. Indignation has taken hold of me because of the wicked, who forsake Your law. Your statutes have been my songs in the house of my pilgrimage. I remember Your name in the night, O Lord, and I keep Your law. This has become mine, because I kept Your precepts.

In John 8:31, 32, it sets us free: "Then Jesus said to those Jews who believed Him, 'If you abide in My word, you are My disciples indeed. And you shall know the truth, and the truth shall make you free.' "

In John 15:3 and 17:17, it cleans us up: "You are already clean because of the word which I have spoken to you." "Sanctify them by Your truth. Your word is truth."

71

of God's Word to influence lives for
e measured. In the true story of *Mutiny*
~~~~~, we see this power displayed. Nine
mutineers, six native men, and 12 Tahitian women
and children went ashore at Pitcairn Island in the year
1790. Their lifestyles soon fell into chaos, and when
one sailor began distilling alcohol, the little colony
was further plunged into debauchery and vice.

Within 10 years, only one white man survived, surrounded by native women and children born in
depravity. Then one day in an old chest, the sailor
found a Bible. He began to read it and later to teach
it to the others. The result was that his own life, and
ultimately the lives of all those left in the colony,
were changed. In 1808, a ship discovered Pitcairn
Island and found that it had become prosperous,
with no jail, no whiskey, no crime and no laziness.
The Bible is alive and active.

Different in Its Penetration

"For the word of God is living and powerful, and
sharper than any two-edged sword, piercing even to
the division of soul and spirit" (Hebrews 4:12).

The Word of God is a two-edged sword. The Holy
Spirit uses this sword. It is available to us as the
offensive weapon in spiritual warfare. "And take the
helmet of salvation, and the sword of the Spirit,
which is the word of God" (Ephesians 6:17).

Throughout Scripture, the voice of the Lord is
described as a sword. In Isaiah 49:2, a prophecy concerning Jesus is given, stating, "He has made My

mouth like a sharp sword." In Revelation 1:16 and 19:15, Jesus is pictured as having a sword coming from His mouth.

The penetration of the Word into the dividing of soul and spirit speaks of the conversion experience. Man is body (physical life), soul (mental life) and spirit (spiritual life). Until one is saved, his spirit is dead, entombed within the soul. In the fall of Adam, the spirit of man was separated from God and death was the result.

The lost man is referred to as "the natural man" in 1 Corinthians 2:14. The word for *natural* in the Greek is the same word as *soul*. When the Word of God penetrates our souls, it divides the spirit of man from the tomb of his own soul. Once that takes place, the Spirit of God rules the spirit of the man; thus, a takeover of the soul and body becomes possible. This is a beautiful picture of what happens on the inside when we are saved. The expression "joints and marrow" speaks of the external and internal work of the Word of God.

The spirit of man that is separated from God and spiritual life is governed by the body (flesh-life) as well as the soul (intellectual life). A lost person is world-conscious until the Word penetrates his or her life.

As a Christian, you will never be *spiritual* until the sword of the Word of God enters your life and cuts away that which does not belong.

Many years ago, a young man named Lew Wallace journeyed to the Middle East and Southern Europe to write a book refuting the Bible. As he read the Bible and other writings to research for his book, his heart began to be stirred. Before he could finish writing his own book, he was brought under conviction and gloriously saved. He immediately changed the focus of his book, and the classic *Ben Hur* was birthed. The Word of God can cut through intellectual arguments and bring a doubter to Christ!

Different in Its Revelation

God knows our hearts! The Word of God reveals our thoughts. Have you ever thought that a pastor or evangelist was speaking directly to you during a sermon or address? The Word of God was actually moving in your thoughts. Furthermore, God's Word reveals your intentions or motives. If our motives or intentions are self-directed and wrong, the Word exposes our sin.

God's Word shows all of us that nothing can be hidden from God. His Word illuminates the dark corners of our hearts. Every secret sin and every skeleton in the closet is exposed before the eyes of the Almighty. Make no mistake about it, God knows you inside and out.

CONCLUSION

These truths concerning God's powerful Word should arrest the Christian's attention. One commentator stated that the Bible deserves our careful consideration, our constant meditation and a complete application to our lives. I would add that the Word

of God needs to be declared to those around us.
Where the Bible is declared, there is life and hope.
Where the Word of God is ignored or unknown,
there is darkness and death.

Over 160 years ago, four Indians from west of the
Rocky Mountains traveled 3,000 miles to St. Louis.
Upon arriving at the doorstep of General William
Clark, the superintendent of Indian Affairs, two of
the Native men dropped dead from sickness and
exhaustion. The two remaining Indians were treated
with much fanfare and given a tour of the local sites,
including places of entertainment and local Catholic
churches. For a while, the purpose of the Indians'
visit was not clear. Finally they revealed that they had
heard of "The White Man's Book of Life," and had
come "to hunt for it" and "to ask for teachers to be
sent" to their tribe.

At the close of their visit in St. Louis, one of the
Indians named Ta-Wis-Sis-Sim-Nim stood at a farewell
banquet and dictated the following:

My people sent me to get the white man's Book of
Heaven. You took me where you allow your women
to dance, as we do not ours; and the Book was not
there! You took me to where they worship the Great
Spirit with candles, and the Book was not there! You
showed me images of the Great Spirit and pictures of
the Good Land beyond, but the Book was not among
them to tell me the way. I am going back the long
trail to my people in the dark land. You make my feet
heavy with gifts, and my moccasins will grow old in

carrying them, and yet the Book is not among them! When I tell my poor blind people, after one more snow, in the big council, that I did not bring the Book, no word will be spoken by our old men or by our young braves. One by one, they will rise up and go out in silence. My people will die in darkness, and they will go a long path to other hunting grounds. No white man will go with them, and no white man's Book to make the way plain. I have no more words.

The Indian's parting speech was published in an 1833 issue of *Christian Advocate and Journal*. As a result, the hearts of many of God's people were stirred with conviction that such an opportunity to share the truth was so tragically neglected. Approximately 100 missionaries responded to the call of Native missions. Among them were Marcus and Narcissa Whitman, who were martyred on the field.

People today are still hungry for the guidance and living water found in the Word of God. We must not grow weary in reaching them with the powerful truth of salvation in Christ.

8

What Is Jesus Doing Now?

Seeing then that we have a great High Priest who has passed through the heavens, Jesus the Son of God, let us hold fast our confession. For we do not have a High Priest who cannot sympathize with our weaknesses, but was in all points tempted as we are, yet without sin. Let us therefore come boldly to the throne of grace, that we may obtain mercy and find grace to help in time of need. For every high priest taken from among men is appointed for men in things pertaining to God, that he may offer both gifts and sacrifices for sins. He can have compassion on those who are ignorant and going astray, since he himself is also subject to weakness. Because of this he is required as for the people, so also for himself, to offer sacrifices for sins. And no man takes this honor to himself, but he who is called by God, just as Aaron was. So also Christ did not glorify Himself to become High Priest, but it was He who said to Him: "You are My Son, today I have begotten You." As He also says in another place: "You are a priest forever according to the order of Melchizedek"; who, in the days of His flesh, when He had offered up prayers and supplications, with vehement cries and tears to Him who was able to save Him from death, and was heard because of His godly fear, though He was a Son, yet He learned obedience by the things which He suffered. And having been perfected, He became the author of eternal salvation to all who obey Him, called by God as High Priest "according to the order of Melchizedek" (Hebrews 4:14—5:10).

INTRODUCTION

In the Book of Hebrews, Jesus has already been identified as our Great High Priest. In 2:17, 18, He is identified as our "merciful and faithful High Priest." In 3:1, He is called "the Apostle and High Priest of our confession." Chapters 1—4 of Hebrews have been concerned with the supreme Word of our Great High Priest. Now we come to the supreme Work of the Great High Priest.

In the previous passage, we observed the power of the "sword of the Spirit." This is the instrument of sacrifice. Hebrews 4 pictures the work of the priest in offering a sacrifice. After the priest examined the animal outwardly, it would be cut open and examined inwardly before the sacrifice was offered and accepted by God.

The Word of God is a sword in the hand of our High Priest, who examines not only our outward appearance, but reveals a clear view of the needs, sins and weaknesses of our hearts. This is a terrifying thought until we read the following verses. Then we see the mighty work of our Lord as the Great High Priest.

A priest was one who represented man before God. Jesus was not just a priest of a son of Aaron. He was not merely part of some earthly order of high priests who were annually appointed. He has been named "Great High Priest," a title never bestowed on any other. It is this work that Jesus began on earth and continues to this very day. Note the marks of His priesthood.

He Is a Sovereign Priest (v. 14)

The phrase "who has passed through the heavens" speaks of His glorious ascension to the right hand of the Father. When He ascended, Jesus conquered the throngs of hell. Satan is called the "prince of the power of the air" (Ephesians 2:2). When Jesus ascended, the forces of hell had to bow.

Can you imagine the scene on the day of Jesus' ascension? The disciples and about 500 others watched as Jesus began to rise. Up He went through the stratosphere and ionosphere of our planet. Up He went past the moon and the planets of our solar system as they salute their Creator. Up He ascended beyond the Milky Way, as the starry hosts applauded in an explosion of brilliant light. Finally, in ascended glory, He took His place at the Father's right hand where "He always lives to make intercession for us" (Hebrews 7:25).

He Is a Sympathetic Priest (4:15—5:3)

These are comforting promises. We see that Jesus knows us better than we know ourselves, and He still loves us!

He knows our nature (4:15). We have weaknesses inherent in our human nature. Jesus became one of us. He experienced our weaknesses. He knew what it was to be lonely, to hurt, to weep, to be utterly fatigued, hungry and thirsty, and to be rejected. Furthermore, He was tempted in every possible way by Satan, and yet did not sin.

He knows our need (4:16—5:3). The Lord is enthroned on a seat of grace. From there He reaches to help us with our needs. These encouraging words in Hebrews furnish us with a beautiful portrait of the work of our Great High Priest. Though the throne represents authority, it is gracious authority. The Lord left the throne of glory to sit upon a throne of grace. Those who will not come before His throne of grace will one day have to stand before the Great White Throne of grief. In the end, Jesus again will take the throne of government and glory.

The marks of a faithful priest are given in Hebrews 5:1-3. The true Priest is an intercessor for others. The true Priest has compassion on the spiritually ignorant and the lost. The true Priest meets the needs of others. Human priests had to offer sacrifices for themselves as well as the people, but Jesus, being perfect, had no need to do that. Jesus offered Himself for our needs. He cares for us and still meets our needs daily as we come to His throne of grace.

> He knows the bitter weary way;
> The endless striving day by day;
> He knows how hard the fight has been,
> The clouds that cover our lives between,

The wounds the world has never seen,
He knows, Oh thought so full of bliss!
For though on earth our joys we miss,
We can still bear it feeling this.
He knows!

—G.W. Lyons

It is encouraging to know that He sees our every thought and motive with complete understanding. It is a great comfort to be assured that He cares.

He Is a Suffering Priest (5:5-8)

In the old covenant, the priest brought a sacrifice, but in the new covenant, our Great High Priest became the sacrifice Himself. In these verses, we study His voluntary sacrifice. He was obedient and submissive to the Father, even in the Garden of Gethsemane, the place of agony. There He faced the supreme crisis of His life. There the dreaded cup of our sins was first pressed against His sinless lips—a cup that would be fully drained at Calvary.

Our Lord was our Priest by divine appointment. The Father chose Him, and Jesus was an obedient Son. Verse 7 brings us near our Lord during His dark hour in Gethsemane. *Prayers* (*deesis*) and *supplications* (*hiketerias*) are not the usual Greek words for praying. *Prayer* has to do with a request made out of great need. *Supplication* refers to a call for urgent aid. Because the Savior cried out to the Father in the depths of His need, He can meet our needs for all eternity, even sealing our souls in mercy.

His prayer was to be saved, not *from* dying, but *out* of death. Jesus was praying to the Father, looking forward to the Resurrection.

As the Lord Jesus suffered the pain we deserved, He was weeping and crying out loud. He obeyed the Father and took on our sins. The Father heard His prayers and Christ arose from the dead. Now the Father hears the prayer of the Son in our stead. Charles Wesley best defined the present-day role and relationship of God the Father and God the Son when he penned the classic hymn, "Arise My Soul, Arise":

> Five bleeding wounds He bears, received on Calvary;
> They pour effectual prayers, they strongly plead for me;
> "Forgive Him, O forgive," they cry,
> "Nor let the ransomed sinner die!"
> The Father hears Him pray, His dear anointed One;
> He cannot turn away the presence of His Son.

He Is a Saving Priest (5:9, 10)

He was "made perfect" (v. 9, KJV). This refers to the absolute fulfillment of every part of His work. He completed the work through His sacrifice.

Because of this, He is now the source of our eternal salvation. Salvation is God's total work of delivering a human being from the *penalty* of sin, from the *power* of sin, and one day from the *presence* of sin. This salvation is found in Jesus Christ alone.

One mark of that salvation is that it belongs to those who are obedient. Just as Jesus obediently surrendered to the Father, the lost person must surrender in obedience to Jesus as Lord.

Jesus is an eternal priest, not a temporary one like Aaron was. Melchizedek was a royal priest after the eternal heavenly order. Jesus is our eternal High Priest forever. Right now He is praying for us.

> Therefore He is also able to save to the uttermost those who come to God through Him, since He always lives to make intercession for them (Hebrews 7:25).

> My little children, these things I write to you, so that you may not sin. And if anyone sins, we have an Advocate with the Father, Jesus Christ the righteous (1 John 2:1).

CONCLUSION

Having this Great High Priest, our Lord Jesus Christ, what are we told to do?

"Let us hold fast our confession" (Hebrews 4:14). We are not to allow the temptation and testing of this life to draw us away from Christ.

"Let us therefore come boldly to the throne of grace" (v. 16). We are to come to God with our needs and burdens, feeling the freedom to speak to Him. We can open our hearts, for with Him we will find help in time of need—"in the nick of time" as we say today. Jesus is always there to help just when we need it most.

Don't be afraid to come to His throne of grace and mercy . . . draw near today!

9

The Anchor
of the Soul

Of whom we have much to say, and hard to explain, since you have become dull of hearing. For though by this time you ought to be teachers, you need someone to teach you again the first principles of the oracles of God; and you have come to need milk and not solid food. For everyone who partakes only of milk is unskilled in the word of righteousness, for he is a babe. But solid food belongs to those who are of full age, that is, those who by reason of use have their senses exercised to discern both good and evil. Therefore, leaving the discussion of the elementary principles of Christ, let us go on to perfection, not laying again the foundation of repentance from dead works and of faith toward God, of the doctrine of baptisms, of laying on of hands, of resurrection of the dead, and of eternal judgment. And this we will do if God permits. For it is impossible for those who were once enlightened, and have tasted the heavenly gift, and have become partakers of the Holy Spirit, and have tasted the good word of God and the powers of the age to come, if they fall away, to renew them again to repentance, since they crucify again for themselves the Son of God, and put Him to an open shame. For the earth which drinks in the rain that often comes upon it, and bears herbs useful for those by whom it is cultivated, receives blessing from God; but if it bears thorns and briars, it is rejected and near to being cursed, whose end is to be burned. But, beloved, we are confident of better things concerning you, yes, things that accompany salvation, though we speak in this manner. For God is not unjust to forget your work and labor of love which you have shown toward His name, in that you have ministered to the saints, and do minister. And we desire that each one of you show the same diligence to the full assurance of hope until the end, that you do not become sluggish, but imitate those who through faith and patience inherit the promises. For when God made a promise to Abraham, because He could swear by no one greater, He swore by Himself, saying, "Surely blessing I will bless you, and multiplying I will multiply you." And so, after he had patiently endured, he obtained the promise. For men indeed swear by the greater, and an oath for confirmation is for them an end of all dispute. Thus God, determining to show more abundantly to the heirs of promise the immutability of His counsel, confirmed it by an oath, that by two immutable things, in which it is impossible for God to lie, we might have strong consolation, who have fled for refuge to lay hold of the hope set before us. This hope we have as an anchor of the soul, both sure and steadfast, and which enters the Presence behind the veil, where the forerunner has entered for us, even Jesus, having become High Priest forever according to the order of Melchizedek (Hebrews 5:11—6:20).

INTRODUCTION

Where can a human being find security in uncertain days? According to Hebrews, our security is found in Jesus Christ. On earth He is our help, and in heaven He is our hope.

A traveler to Greece in our day observed the Parthenon being cleaned. The worker doing the cleaning commented to the tourists, "You know, what 25 centuries could not do to this beautiful structure, the corrosive breath of the 21st century is quickly doing!"

Our nation is suffering from the corrosive immoral breath of the 21st century. The secularism, humanism, materialism, liberalism and commercialism of our day have devastated our sources of security. The home, once the primary place of stability, has become a battleground. The church has forfeited its power because of worldliness.

Modern living is rooted in false philosophies. Just before his death, Bertrand Russell, one of the most noted logicians of the past century, made a dramatic statement: "All the labor of the ages, all devotions, all the inspiration, all the noonday brightness of human genius are destined to extinction in the vast death of the solar system." He goes on to say the soul's habitation is nothing but unyielding despair.

Many Christians live with despair, a lack of assurance and insecurity. This passage in Hebrews sets forth the enemies and essentials of hope. It is vitally important in a world shrouded in hopelessness, that there is a strong testimony from those who have found hope in Christ. Hebrews 6:11 says that we ought to "show . . . the full assurance of hope until the end." In order to do that, we must deal with the enemies of assurance.

The Enemies of Assurance (5:11—6:8)

Two reasons stand out concerning why people do not live in assurance.

1. *Immaturity* (5:11—6:3). These verses are a stinging rebuke to lazy Christianity. In verse 11, the word *dull* would better be translated "lazy or slothful." It portrays an "I-don't-care" attitude toward the Word of God.

In verse 12, this laziness toward the Word resulted in uselessness to the cause of Christ. The believers, who ought to be teaching others, are still unable to grasp the basics of the Christian life. In verses 13 and 14, we see that their lives are characterized by worldliness. God's Word is a "word of righteousness." Those who are growing in Christ are sensitive to evil—they know what is right or wrong.

For growth, two things are essential: in the physical realm, you must have proper diet and exercise. The believer needs the same things spiritually. Solid food and exercise are needed to keep spiritually healthy. In verse 14, the word *practice* or *exercise* translates from the Greek word *gumnazo,* from which our word *gymnasium* comes. The Word of God must be absorbed and practiced in order to build a strong Christian life.

Not until we grow up can we go onward (6:1-3). The passage indicates that we should literally be borne along. Mature Christians are carried along by the power of God. We must move on from the foundations of our faith into building a life of faith.

2. *Insincerity* (vv. 4-8). Some people doubt because they have never had a genuine salvation experience.

These verses have been most controversial. Some who believe that one may be saved and lost again point out that the terms "enlightened," "tasted of the heavenly gift," and "shared in the Holy Spirit" describe more than a dabbler in spiritual things. If understood literally, these verses say there was a definite time in the past when these persons shared in the grace of God, something more than temporary religious enthusiasm.

According to this view, the description is of men who had experienced the joy of salvation, the fellowship of the Spirit, the nourishment and satisfaction of the Word, and the confirmation of the supernatural. Just as it is possible to willfully decide to follow Christ, it is possible to willfully decide to turn away from Him.

Others—I among them—believe these verses portray a counterfeit Christian. This entire passage of Scripture is similar to what Jesus taught in the parable of the wheat and tares.

Notice what these counterfeits had received. They had seen the light, tasted the Spirit of God and the Word of God, and experienced miracles. Yet they had fallen away, or more literally interpreted, "fallen alongside."

These people made professions of faith and had been a part of the church. Now they rejected what they had professed. Their rejection was so absolute that there stood no possibility of repentance. Like the Jewish nation, they so utterly rejected Christ that it was like a second crucifixion.

First John 2:19 says, "They went out from us, but they were not of us; for if they had been of us, they would have continued with us; but they went out that they might be made manifest, that none of them were of us."

Hebrews 6:7, 8 reminds us of the parable of the wheat and the tares. Those who made insincere decisions would show it by the fruit of their lives. Their product would be thorns and thistles ready to be burned!

Let me warn you—if you have never trusted Christ, do it now before the rejection becomes so final and your heart so hard that you cannot respond.

The Essentials of Assurance (6:9-20)

How can we live in security and assurance? As we grow in maturity, going on in our spiritual pilgrimage, we discover three truths that anchor the soul in hope.

Stand on the Promises (vv. 9-18). These verses declare that true Christians will continue to serve the Lord regardless of what may happen outwardly. The sincere believer stands on the promises of God. We are heirs to all the promises of God (vv. 11, 12).

Abraham is given as an illustration of an "heir of God." God had promised to bless Abraham and multiply his seed through Isaac. God again gives the promise meaning through the authority of His Word. When God makes a promise, nothing can break it! It is impossible for God to lie.

When God spoke peace to my heart through Jesus, He promised me life eternal. Nothing can break that promise. R. Kelso Carter expressed this in his great hymn:

> Standing on the promises that cannot fail,
> When the howling storms of doubt and fear assail;
> By the living Word of God I shall prevail,
> Standing on the promises of God.

Hiding in the Refuge (v. 18). The phrase found here, "who have fled for refuge," takes us back to Numbers 35:6 and the cities of refuge in the Old Testament:

> "Now among the cities which you will give to the Levites you shall appoint six cities of refuge, to which a manslayer may flee. And to these you shall add forty-two cities."

It was to these cities that an accused person could flee and be protected until given a fair trial. Our city of refuge is the Lord Jesus Christ. I have fled to Him from my sins and from the wrath to come. I can hide in Jesus and be protected forevermore. Assurance comes when we know that we are protected in the refuge of Jesus.

Be Anchored to the Forerunner (6:19, 20). The Greek word for *hope* is *elpis*. It means "an anchor rope." In past times, every harbor had great stones that were embedded in the ground near the water's edge. These stones served as moorings for the sailing vessels. Sometimes the ships could not make it to the moorings under their own sail. In such cases a "forerunner" would go ashore in a small boat with a line that would be tied on to the anchor rock. When the rope was firmly fastened, those on the ship would pull the ship to shore with the anchor rope.

Our Lord Jesus, the great forerunner, has gone into glory and tied the rope of our salvation to His throne. Though we cannot see that rope, it is tied firmly to the Rock of Ages. Thank God for the unseen certainty, our hope in Jesus Christ.

CONCLUSION

There is only one hope according to Ephesians 4:4—"one hope of your calling." That hope is our armor—"and as a helmet the hope of salvation" (1 Thessalonians 5:8). Our hope is alive—"a living hope" (1 Peter 1:3). Our hope abides eternally, as 1 Corinthians 13:13 states, "Now abide faith, hope, love." Hope is the anchor of the soul!

When everything seems to be out of sorts, when death comes to call, when difficulties arise—at that moment we can find ourselves safely anchored in the Rock of Strength, Jesus.

10

The Mystery of Melchizedek

For this Melchizedek, king of Salem, priest of the Most High God, who met Abraham returning from the slaughter of the kings and blessed him, to whom also Abraham gave a tenth part of all, first being translated "king of righteousness," and then also king of Salem, meaning "king of peace," without father, without mother, without genealogy, having neither beginning of days nor end of life, but made like the Son of God, remains a priest continually. Now consider how great this man was, to whom even the patriarch Abraham gave a tenth of the spoils. And indeed those who are of the sons of Levi, who receive the priesthood, have a commandment to receive tithes from the people according to the law, that is, from their brethren, though they have come from the loins of Abraham; but he whose genealogy is not derived from them received tithes from Abraham and blessed him who had the promises. Now beyond all contradiction the lesser is blessed by the better. Here mortal men receive tithes, but there he receives them, of whom it is witnessed that he lives. Even Levi, who receives tithes, paid tithes through Abraham, so to speak, for he was still in the loins of his father when Melchizedek met him. Therefore, if perfection were through the Levitical priesthood (for under it the people received the law), what further need was there that another priest should rise according to the order of Melchizedek, and not be called according to the order of Aaron? For the priesthood being changed, of necessity there is also a change of the law. For He of whom these things are spoken belongs to another tribe, from which no man has officiated at the altar. For it is evident that our Lord arose from Judah, of which tribe Moses spoke nothing concerning priesthood. And it is yet far more evident if, in the likeness of Melchizedek, there arises another priest who has come, not according to the law of a fleshly commandment, but according to the power of an endless life. For He testifies: "You are a priest forever according to the order of Melchizedek." For on the one hand there is an annulling of the former commandment because of its weakness and unprofitableness, for the law made nothing perfect; on the other hand, there is the bringing in of a better hope, through which we draw near to God. And inasmuch as He was not made priest without an oath (for they have become priests without an oath, but He with an oath by Him who said to Him: "The Lord has sworn and will not relent, 'You are a priest forever according to the order of Melchizedek'"), by so much more Jesus has become a surety of a better covenant. Also there were many priests, because they were prevented by death from continuing. But He, because He continues forever, has an unchangeable priesthood. Therefore He is also able to save to the uttermost those who come to God through Him, since He always lives to make intercession for them. For such a High Priest was fitting for us, who is holy, harmless, undefiled, separate from sinners, and has become higher than the heavens; who does not need daily, as those high priests, to offer up sacrifices, first for His own sins and then for the people's, for this He did once for all when He offered up Himself. For the law appoints as high priests men who have weakness, but the word of the oath, which came after the law, appoints the Son who has been perfected forever (Hebrews 7:1-28).

INTRODUCTION

In the ancient account of Job, we find a poignant passage where the deep longings of Job's heart are expressed: his desire for an audience with the Almighty. You can truly hear his heart in these verses: "For He is not a man, as I am, that I may answer Him, and that we should go to court together. Nor is there any mediator between us, who may lay his hand on us both" (Job 9:32, 33).

What Job longed for most was a Great High Priest who was both God and man. What Job cried for was fulfillment in Jesus Christ. He is our Great High Priest, who stands in the Father's presence on our behalf to ensure our connection to the Father.

The Book of Hebrews declares this glorious truth. In 2:17, Jesus is called our "merciful and faithful High Priest." In 4:15, 16, we read that Christ was "in all points tempted as we are, yet without sin . . . that we may obtain mercy and find grace to help in time of need."

The Hebrews would respond to this by saying, "We already have a priesthood: the Aaronic and Levitical priesthood. This Jesus is not in the priestly line. How can He be our High Priest?" As we will learn, the mysterious Melchizedek answers that question. This intriguing historical character prefigures Christ's priesthood in three specific ways.

THIS ORDER WAS SHROUDED IN MYSTERY (7:3)

Melchizedek appears suddenly in Genesis 14 after Abraham had defeated the great king of Elam, Chedorlaomer. When Melchizedek showed up, Abraham chose to honor this king-priest. The priest was from the city of Salem, which, according to the historian Josephus, is the ancient name of Jerusalem.

Hebrews 7:3 declares that Melchizedek was not a priest by descent, but by divine call. The phrase here does not mean that he did not have a father or mother. It means that he did not have a genealogy.

Furthermore, the mystery about this king-priest deepens when we read in 7:3 that Melchizedek was "made like the Son of God." Jesus was not a reflection of Melchizedek; rather, Melchizedek was like Jesus. God called this man out and gave him a ministry that was filled with hope, much like the mission Jesus would proclaim years later. No wonder Jesus said, "Your father Abraham rejoiced to see My day" (John 8:56). When Abraham saw Mechizedek, he saw one like Jesus.

THIS ORDER IS STRONGER IN MINISTRY (7:1-2)

Melchizedek is mentioned in one other Old Testament passage, Psalm 110. This great psalm is quoted several times in Hebrews (1:13; 5:6; 6:20; 7:17, 21). This particular psalm is a prophecy of the coming of Jesus into the world, and declares that the Messiah's priesthood would be after the order of Melchizedek (Psalm 110:4).

In the Genesis 14 account, Abraham had just returned from a great victory over four kings. He had rescued his nephew Lot and the king of Sodom, and the grateful king was about to offer riches to Abraham. God knew that Abraham would need strength to face that temptation, so He sent the king of Salem, Melchizedek.

In Genesis 14:18, Melchizedek brought bread and wine. These were the symbols of the price of victory. Both body and blood were sacrificed when a victory was obtained. Melchizedek came out to remind Abraham that it was the Most High God, El Elyon, who had given him the victory. Melchizedek then blessed Abraham, and Abraham gave a tithe to God as a recognition of God's ownership of everything in his life.

The king of Sodom had intended to offer Abraham worldly riches. God sent this king-priest to remind Abraham the true meaning of wealth and victory. Because Abraham refused to take credit for the victory and turned down the reward of the world, God appeared to him and said, "Do not be afraid, Abram. I am your shield, your exceedingly great reward" (Genesis 15:1).

That ancient ministry is a beautiful picture of the ministry of our Lord Jesus. He is our King of Righteousness, and when we receive Him, He also becomes our King of Peace. Christ is the source of our victory. Each time a church fellowship shares the bread and the wine of Holy Communion, it remembers Jesus' victory on Calvary, which gives us victory today. It is to Him and not to the world that we owe our loyalty.

From this story, we also learn that our tithes are an acknowledgment of His victory and ownership of all. Abraham tithed long before God set forth the laws of giving and tithing! Today we pay homage to our King Jesus with our tithes.

THIS ORDER IS SUPERIOR IN MAJESTY (7:4-28)

These verses show the superiority of the Melchizedek priesthood. In doing so, they also define the Levitical priesthood and declare the majesty of the Lord Jesus Christ. In Hebrews 7, we find three declarations that proclaim His majesty.

1. *He lives forever* (vv. 4-24). The thrust of these verses is that the priesthood of Jesus is superior because He never needs to be replaced. He does not die and thus serves as a priest continually (vv. 8, 14-17, 21, 24). The Levitical priests held their office by genealogy, but our Lord was Priest by divine oath (vv. 11-17). The old priesthood was subject to weakness because of death, and thus was set aside (vv. 18-23). But our Lord lives on forever to remain our High Priest.

2. *He saves forever* (vv. 24, 25). He saves forever those who come to God by Him. What a simple verse on salvation! Being "saved" is simply coming to God through Jesus. We are saved forever because Jesus never stops interceding for us. The word *intercede* (Greek: *entugchano*) means "to entreat in favor of." The Lord continually represents us at the Father's throne.

3. *He reigns forever* (vv. 26-28). He is the eternal sacrifice (vv. 26, 27). Our Lord who went down to death for us has now been exalted to the highest throne of the heavens. Unlike the priests of the Old Testament who daily offered sacrifices, our Lord offered Himself once and for all.

> Not all the blood of beasts on Jewish altars slain,
> Could give the guilty conscience peace, Or take away
>   our stain.
> But Christ, the heavenly lamb, takes all our sins away.
> A sacrifice of nobler name, and richer blood, than they.
> —Isaac Watts

His great sacrifice stretches from eternity to eternity, because He is the beloved Son (v. 28).

Human priests were subject to the infirmities and frailties caused by their sin natures. They would die and their service ended. Jesus was consecrated as High Priest by the oath of the Father. Perhaps that was the consecration that took place at His baptism when the Father said, "This is My beloved Son, in whom I am well pleased" (Matthew 3:17). Though Jesus our Great High Priest died, He arose to an eternal ministry.

99

CONCLUSION

When you come under the reign of Jesus, the King of Righteousness, you can know Him as your peace. Psalm 85:10 reveals that "righteousness and peace have kissed." To know real peace, you must first repent of sin and receive His righteousness. The Bible says, "'There is no peace,' says my God, 'for the wicked'" (Isaiah 57:21).

Jesus' parable of the prodigal son told how one boy learned this lesson. The wayward son could not receive the kiss of peace and welcome from his father until he left his sin behind and came home. May righteousness and peace kiss each other in your life.

11

God's New Deal

Now this is the main point of the things we are saying: We have such a High Priest, who is seated at the right hand of the throne of the Majesty in the heavens, a Minister of the sanctuary and of the true tabernacle which the Lord erected, and not man. For every high priest is appointed to offer both gifts and sacrifices. Therefore it is necessary that this One also have something to offer. For if He were on earth, He would not be a priest, since there are priests who offer the gifts according to the law; who serve the copy and shadow of the heavenly things, as Moses was divinely instructed when he was about to make the tabernacle. For He said, "See that you make all things according to the pattern shown you on the mountain." But now He has obtained a more excellent ministry, inasmuch as He is also Mediator of a better covenant, which was established on better promises. For if that first covenant had been faultless, then no place would have been sought for a second. Because finding fault with them, He says: "Behold, the days are coming, says the Lord, when I will make a new covenant with the house of Israel *and with the house of Judah—not according to the covenant that I made with their fathers in the day when I took them by the hand to lead them out of the land of Egypt; because they did not continue in My covenant, and I disregarded them, says the Lord. For this is the covenant that I will make with the house of Israel after those days, says the Lord: I will put My laws in their mind and write them on their hearts; and I will be their God, and they shall be My people. None of them shall teach his neighbor, and none his brother, saying, 'Know the Lord,' for all shall know Me, from the least of them to the greatest of them. For I will be merciful to their unrighteousness, and their sins and their lawless deeds I will remember no more." In that He says, "A new covenant," He has made the first obsolete. Now what is becoming obsolete and growing old is ready to vanish away* (Hebrews 8:1-13).

INTRODUCTION

In these verses we catch a glimpse of Jesus' heavenly work. It is exciting to know that at this very moment, One who bears the scars of His love represents us in heaven. The One who walked the dusty trails of Israel, died on the cross, arose from the dead, and ascended on high is now our Mediator with God.

Hebrews 8:1 declares that this is the *sum* (KJV) or "crowning point" of Hebrews. The *New King James Version* translates *sum* as "the main point." The crowning point is that our Lord Jesus lives in glory as our Priest, Mediator, Minister, Forerunner and Intercessor.

As such, He has fulfilled the shadows and scriptures of the old covenant and brought a new covenant to God's people. When Franklin Roosevelt was running for president, he promised a "New Deal." That promise could not even remotely compare to God's new deal! Three aspects of this new covenant should be studied.

The Priest of the New Covenant (8:1-3)

The Great High Priest stands apart from any other.

He is a Saving Priest. The Christian can stand in gratitude for the salvation provided by our Great High Priest, because He has ransomed our souls from eternal punishment.

He is a Seated Priest. Nowhere in the Old Testament do we see the Levitical priest seated. Hebrews 10:11 states, "And every priest stands ministering daily and offering repeatedly the same sacrifices." Their work was never finished, but Jesus' work was completed on the cross.

He is a Sovereign Priest. Our Lord sits in heaven, fully man and fully God, in all the matchless dignity He so richly deserves. Nothing remains to be done for our salvation. Nothing else needs to be done, for the Lord sits on the throne of grace with the absolute authority to save.

He is a Serving Priest. At first glance, this would seem to be contradictory. He is seated, but serving! The word *service,* or *minister* (v. 2), is the Greek word *leitourgos,* which is the same word from which we get our word *liturgy* and refers to our "order of worship." Jesus, seated at the right hand of God, had authority to give order and keep order in worship. Paul tells us in Romans 12:1 that we are to "present [our] bodies a living sacrifice, holy, acceptable to God, which is [our] reasonable service." Jesus offers us to the Father as we offer ourselves to Him. He has made the supreme offering by which we may offer ourselves to Him.

The Prophecy of the New Covenant (8:4-9)

Two prophecies of the new covenant are found in this passage.

The Old Testament Sanctuary (vv. 4, 5). As we studied earlier, the Tabernacle of the Old Testament was built according to the pattern given to Moses. Exodus 25:40 is quoted in Hebrews 8:5, "Moses was divinely instructed when he was about to make the tabernacle. For He said, 'See that you make all things according to the pattern shown you on the mountain.'" Even the earthly place of worship was just a copy of the true sanctuary in heaven where Jesus now sits.

Little did the Jews know that their holy place would be completely destroyed by the Romans less than 100 years after this was written. How foolish of these Hebrew Christians to trust in a building that was only a shadow of that to come. Verse 13 declares that the old covenant, including its sanctuary, was ready to vanish.

This is a good warning to us today—we should guard ourselves against trusting building, rituals, denomination or church membership in the place of knowing Christ.

The Old Testament Scripture. The great prophet Jeremiah, on the eve of another prophesied destruction of Jerusalem, predicted the coming of a new covenant. The writer of Hebrews (8:8-12) quotes Jeremiah 31:31-34:

> "Behold, the days are coming, says the Lord, when I will make a new covenant with the house of Israel and with the house of Judah—not according to the covenant that I made with their fathers in the day that I took them by the hand to lead them out of the land of Egypt, My covenant which they broke, though I was a husband to them, says the Lord. But this is the covenant that I will make with the house of Israel after those days, says the Lord: I will put My law in their minds, and write it on their hearts; and I will be their God, and they shall be My people. No more shall every man teach his neighbor, and every man his brother, saying, 'Know the Lord,' for they all shall know Me, from the least of them to the greatest of them, says the Lord. For I will forgive their iniquity, and their sin I will remember no more."

This prophecy declares that God is sending something better to His people.

The old covenant (also known as the Mosaic covenant) is referenced here. This covenant of law was conditional and temporary. According to John

Phillips in his book *Exploring Hebrews*, the terms of that covenant were as follows:

- It offered life to those who kept the Law (Exodus 19:1-8).

- It contained the commandments that expressed the righteous will of God (Exodus 20:1-26).

- It contained judgments governing Israel's social life (Exodus 21:1-24)

- It contained ordinances governing Israel's religious life (Exodus 24:12-31; 18).

The old covenant could declare what was wrong, but it could not correct it. It was a stop sign, not a road map! It could condemn, but it could not save. God provided for this in the new covenant.

The Principles of the New Covenant (Hebrews 8:10-13)

The new covenant is based on what God can do, not upon what man may fail to do. Romans 8:3 declares that the law was weakened by our flesh. "For what the law could not do in that it was weak through the flesh, God did by sending His own Son in the likeness of sinful flesh, on account of sin: He condemned sin in the flesh." We could not keep the law, and so we were doomed. Yet God made provision for us in His Son.

The new covenant is inward and spiritual. God does something inside those whom He saves. External rules may control a person, but the rules cannot change a person. God's Word must be written on our hearts.

A new world is promised by the new covenant. We are entered into blessings of the new covenant, but it shall not be complete until we live together as citizens of a redeemed world.

The new covenant also grants us complete pardon from our sin. The old covenant could only cover the sin, not remove it. But Jesus came to "take away the sins of the world" (see John 1:29). God promises not only to forgive but also to forget our sins! He casts them away from memory. "I will forgive their iniquity, and their sin I will remember no more" (Jeremiah 31:34).

CONCLUSION

What you and I need is not a remaking of the old. We don't need a remodeled life—we need a brand-new life. God has a *new deal* for you. He will change you from the inside out if you will trust Him. He takes away the guilt away, and will make you a citizen of a brand-new world where all will know Him in His mercy and grace.

12

The Blood Covenant

Then indeed, even the first covenant had ordinances of divine service and the earthly sanctuary. For a tabernacle was prepared: the first part, in which was the lampstand, the table, and the showbread, which is called the sanctuary; and behind the second veil, the part of the tabernacle which is called the Holiest of All, which had the golden censer and the ark of the covenant overlaid on all sides with gold, in which were the golden pot that had the manna, Aaron's rod that budded, and the tablets of the covenant; and above it were the cherubim of glory overshadowing the mercy seat. Of these things we cannot now speak in detail. Now when these things had been thus prepared, the priests always went into the first part of the tabernacle, performing the services. But into the second part the high priest went alone once a year, not without blood, which he offered for himself and for the people's sins committed in ignorance; the Holy Spirit indicating this, that the way into the Holiest of All was not yet made manifest while the first tabernacle was still standing. It was symbolic for the present time in which both gifts and sacrifices are offered which cannot make him who performed the service perfect in regard to the conscience—concerned only with foods and drinks, various washings, and fleshly ordinances imposed until the time of reformation. But Christ came as High Priest of the good things to come, with the greater and more perfect tabernacle not made with hands, that is, not of this creation. Not with the blood of goats and calves, but with His own blood He entered the Most Holy Place once for all, having obtained eternal redemption. For if the blood of bulls and goats and the ashes of a heifer, sprinkling the unclean, sanctifies for the purifying of the flesh, how much more shall the blood of Christ, who through the eternal Spirit offered Himself without spot to God, cleanse your conscience from dead works to serve the living God? And for this reason He is the Mediator of the new covenant, by means of death, for the redemption of the transgressions under the first covenant, that those who are called may receive the promise of the eternal inheritance. For where there is a testament, there must also of necessity be the death of the testator. For a testament is in force after men are dead, since it has no power at all while the testator lives. Therefore not even the first covenant was dedicated without blood. For when Moses had spoken every precept to all the people according to the law, he took the blood of calves and goats, with water, scarlet wool, and hyssop, and sprinkled both the book itself and all the people, saying, "This is the blood of the covenant which God has commanded you." Then likewise he sprinkled with blood both the tabernacle and all the vessels of the ministry. And according to the law almost all things are purified with blood, and without shedding of blood there is no remission. Therefore it was necessary that the copies of the things in the heavens should be purified with these, but the heavenly things themselves with better sacrifices than these. For Christ has not entered the holy places made with hands, which are copies of the true, but into heaven itself, now to appear in the presence of God for us; not that He should offer Himself often, as the high priest enters the Most Holy Place every year with blood of another—He then would have had to suffer often since the foundation of the world; but now, once at the end of the ages, He has appeared to put away sin by the sacrifice of Himself. And as it is appointed for men to die once, but after this the judgment, so Christ was offered once to bear the sins of many. To those who eagerly wait for Him He will appear a second time, apart from sin, for salvation (Hebrews 9:1-28).

INTRODUCTION

Covenant is the term applied to various transactions made between God and man or between two men. The Hebrew word *berith* means "to cut." Old Testament covenants included an oath and usually was ratified by the slaughtering of an animal. This was an indication that if a party broke the covenant, their fate would be as dire as that of the slain animal.

The old covenant included the Law and the system of blood sacrifices of animals. The transgressor of divine law was subject to the penalty of death.

God provided a system whereby animals could be slain to atone or cover those sins.

The new covenant displaces the old covenant. The New Testament Greek word *diatheke,* meaning "disposition or will," is found here. It is sometimes translated "testament." Our Lord Jesus Christ shed His blood as the offering to ratify the new covenant or testament. This new covenant was His last will and testament. At His death, all the blessings of the new covenant became available to those who believe on Him. Salvation is not merely a decision we make—it is a covenant we enter into.

The issues of salvation are matters of life and death. In this chapter of Hebrews, the word *appear* occurs several times in relationship to Jesus. It is His threefold appearing that guarantees His covenant.

The Ratification of the Covenant (9:1-5, 26)

Christ came to earth to ratify the new covenant. In doing that, He accomplished two things.

He fulfilled the external (vv. 1-10). As we studied earlier, the Tabernacle was a copy or type of the true sanctuary in heaven. The external symbolism of tabernacle worship reflects the true worship that arrived at Christ's coming.

Our Lord Jesus was the New Tabernacle. Like the old, He was more glorious on the inside than on the outside. He is the Bread of Life and the Light of the World pictured by the old Tabernacle items of the table of shewbread and the lampstand. The veil that hung between humanity and the throne of God pointed to Christ's torn flesh (v. 3). Christ was the Ark of the Covenant, bearing perfectly the law of Almighty God. He was the Manna or bread from heaven, just like that which was stored for posterity inside the ark. He is the Source of Life, pre-figured by the budding of Aaron's rod that was also stored in the ark (v. 4). Christ is the Mercy Seat" where sinners can "find grace to help in time of need" (4:16).

All of the Tabernacle worship was temporary and incomplete. The way into the Holy of Holies was restricted (vv. 6-8), because only the high priest could enter once a year, and then only with great ceremony and a covering of blood. The Tabernacle pointed the way, but it could not open the way; only Jesus could do that.

He obtained the eternal (9:11-15, 26). Christ also appeared to obtain that which would never end. The word *appeared* ("came," v. 11) translates from the Greek *paragenomenos,* which means "to come alongside of his own accord once and for all." However, in verse 26, a different word for *appear* is found—*pephanerotai,* which means "to be manifested or to shine forth." The first word signifies a change in conditions, while the second indicates the display of the One who has changed the condition!

Our Lord left the conditions and environment of heaven and became a man. He lived under our earthly and human conditions. Yet, He shined forth with the glory of God. He became subject to the limitations of time so that He might give us eternal life.

By His blood, He obtained "eternal redemption" (v. 12) for us, once and for all. *Redemption* comes from the slave market analogy—He purchased us by His blood in order to set us free.

He offered Himself through the "eternal Spirit" (v. 14). What Jesus came to do was not temporary or repetitive. His offering occurred at one point in time and it lasts forever. The old covenant could not cleanse the conscience, but Jesus cleanses the guilt and sets us free to keep serving God.

By His death, we receive His "eternal inheritance" (v. 15). The riches of the Lord are now ours because of His death. We are recipients of a great inheritance. His blood paid the cost of that great inheritance.

The Preservation of the Covenant (9:10-26)

Verse 24 tells us that Jesus, who appeared on earth to shed His blood for us, now appears in heaven to plead the blood for us. His presence in heaven guarantees the promise of the covenant in two aspects.

1. *The legal guarantee* (vv. 16-22). When Jesus died, His last will and testament came into force. He shed His blood to remove the barriers of our sin and give us the blessings of eternity.

Howard Hughes, who was one of the richest men in the world, left a vast fortune when he died, which many have tried to claim. Unfortunately, he left no will. All the wealth had to be distributed without any knowledge of his wishes.

Not so with Jesus! He designated all His wealth to His children. How foolish we are if we fail to claim our inheritance in Him!

2. *The living guarantee* (vv. 23-26). Our Lord became the sacrifice for our sin. He is a better sacrifice, a sufficient sacrifice and a final sacrifice (vv. 23, 25, 26). Jesus Christ lives, was resurrected, and therefore can enforce the promises of His will. His will is incontestable because He lives in heaven as our guarantee.

The Consummation of the Covenant (9:27, 28)

For years, the world waited for the Messiah to come. Then Christ appeared as a tiny babe, and grew to the Man of Sorrows who died and then rose again for our sins. Today, He appears in heaven as our guarantee (v. 24). One more appearance yet remains—for He shall appear a second time to call us home to heaven.

In the old covenant, on the Day of Atonement, the high priest appeared before the people with the blood of a lamb. He would then go into the Holy of Holies to appear before God with that blood. After placing the blood on the mercy seat, the priest would reappear before the people to bless them. As the priest approached, they could hear the bells on the hem of his robe as he walked, and a great shout of praise would be lifted because they knew God had received the sacrifice.

Our Lord Jesus Christ shall reappear to bless His people, and to take us home to heaven. He is coming for those who are "eagerly expecting Him" (see v. 28).

Just as the Old Testament worshipers awaited the reappearance of the high priest, so should we wait for our Lord's return with hearts of anticipation.

CONCLUSION

All the blessings of the new covenant are ours because of His blood. The blood of Jesus Christ *purchased* our redemption (v. 12), *purged* our conscience (v. 14), *provided* our inheritance (v. 15), *pardoned* our sins (v. 22), *put away* (annulled) our sins (v. 26), and *precluded* our judgment (vv. 27, 28). Hallelujah for the blood!

Today a monument that stands at the location of the World War II Battle of Bastogne reads:

Seldom has so much American blood
been shed in the course of a single action.
Oh Lord, help us remember!

When we go to Calvary and see the blood shed there for us, may we remember and praise His matchless name for the precious gift of life He gave us.

13

Motives for Faithfulness

For the law, having a shadow of the good things to come, and not the very image of the things, can never with these same sacrifices, which they offer continually year by year, make those who approach perfect. For then would they not have ceased to be offered? For the worshipers, once purified, would have had no more consciousness of sins. But in those sacrifices there is a reminder of sins every year. For it is not possible that the blood of bulls and goats could take away sins. Therefore, when He came into the world, He said: "Sacrifice and offering You did not desire, but a body You have prepared for Me. In burnt offerings and sacrifices for sin You had no pleasure. Then I said, 'Behold, I have come—in the volume of the book it is written of Me—to do Your will, O God.'" Previously saying, "Sacrifice and offering, burnt offerings, and offerings for sin You did not desire, nor had pleasure in them" (which are offered according to the law), then He said, "Behold, I have come to do Your will, O God." He takes away the first that He may establish the second. By that will we have been sanctified through the offering of the body of Jesus Christ once for all. And every priest stands ministering daily and offering repeatedly the same sacrifices, which can never take away sins. But this Man, after He had offered one sacrifice for sins forever, sat down at the right hand of God, from that time waiting till His enemies are made His footstool. For by one offering He has perfected forever those who are being sanctified. But the Holy Spirit also witnesses to us; for after He had said before, "This is the covenant that I will make with them after those days, says the Lord: I will put My laws into their hearts, and in their minds I will write them," then He adds, "Their sins and their lawless deeds I will remember no more." Now where there is remission of these, there is no longer an offering for sin. Therefore, brethren, having boldness to enter the Holiest by the blood of Jesus, by a new and living way which He consecrated for us, through the veil, that is, His flesh, and having a High Priest over the house of God, let us draw near with a true heart in full assurance of faith, having our hearts sprinkled from an evil conscience and our bodies washed with pure water. Let us hold fast the confession of our hope without wavering, for He who promised is faithful. And let us consider one another in order to stir up love and good works, not forsaking the assembling of ourselves together, as is the manner of some, but exhorting one another, and so much the more as you see the Day approaching (Hebrews 10:1-25).

INTRODUCTION

Why should those who are believers remain faithful? This passage sets forth the work of Christ with a clear challenge to faithfulness for believers. Jesus entered into a blood covenant with His people. That covenant carries with it certain responsibilities. These responsibilities can be summed up with the word *faithfulness*.

We live in a day of "gypsy" Christianity. This brand of Christianity journeys from one church to another, one conference to another, and never settles into faithful service. However, we are called to be pilgrims, not gypsies! We are journeying together with the people of God.

Over 40 percent of members in an average church never attend services. Among the church's faithful, the average family misses 10 Sundays a year. This is only one of many symptoms of the unfaithfulness that plagues Christians today. Hebrews 10 gives us four driving motivations for faithfulness.

Our Great Salvation (vv. 1-8)

The first motive that stirs our hearts is our great salvation. The sacrificial system of the Old Testament was incomplete. Verse 1 refers to this system as a shadow, which literally means "contour" or "outline." Old Testament religion offered only a faint shadow of the reality of Christ's coming sacrifice.

The sacrifices of the Old Testament were insufficient. Every year they had to be offered, but they never completed the work of atonement. Because of the repeated sacrifices, the worshipers were constantly reminded of their sins (vv. 2-4).

Suppose you had a banker friend who made you pay an annual loan. At the end of the year, you discover you are unable to pay it. So, your friend extends it another year. Year after year, the loan and interest pile up as the note is renewed. This is exactly what was portrayed by the sacrificial system of the Old Testament. Each year, the "note" was delayed another year looking toward Calvary.

That system was inadequate (vv. 5-18). The writer of Hebrews cites Psalm 40:6-8: "Sacrifice and offering You did not desire; my ears You have opened. Burnt offering and sin offering You did not require. Then I said, 'Behold, I come; in the scroll of the book it is written of me. I delight to do Your will, O my God, and Your law is within my heart.'"

This psalm gives us a glimpse of the eternal counsel where the plan of salvation was designed. The Lord Jesus agreed to take a human form and in obedience to the Father offered the final sacrifice for our sins (Hebrews 10:5-10).

As stated before, the sacrifices by the Old Testament priesthood could never take away sins (v. 11). Religious works are inadequate to remove sin. By offering His blood, Jesus paid the debt and made possible a perfect and complete salvation (v. 14). In Him, we are perfectly sanctified (v. 14). That means we are forever cleansed. What Jesus accomplished at the cross continues today.

Furthermore, what God has remitted, He will never remember (vv. 15-18). In this text, Jeremiah 31:33, 34 is quoted again as proof of this full and free pardon. This great salvation calls us to faithfulness.

Our Great Invitation (vv. 10-24)

In the Old Testament Tabernacle, God seemed unapproachable and inaccessible to the average Israelite. Only the high priest was allowed to enter, once a year, in the Holy of Holies where God often was enthroned upon the mercy seat of the ark of the covenant. But our marvelous invitation today is that we can go into the holiest place by the blood of Jesus! We have direct access to God through His blood. Jesus' shed blood opened a way to God for us!

We are called to "draw near with a true heart" (v. 22). This speaks of sincerity in worship. We are to come to Him in full assurance. Our approach to Him can be secure when we come before Him with clean hearts.

Our Great High Priest has invited us to worship Him. He has granted us a continual audience if we desire. We can go in before Him and abide in His glorious presence. Just knowing we are recipients of such a great invitation motivates us to be faithful!

Our Great Obligation (vv. 23-25)

As a part of the family of God, we have an obligation. The first obligation concerns our personal commitments. We are called to "hold fast the confession of our hope" (v. 23). We must not waver in our commitment. Regardless of what may come, believers must stand firm on the confession of hope in Jesus Christ.

The second obligation is to the church, the body of Christ. Verse 24 describes the purpose of church gatherings. Earlier the author described believers as "brothers" in the same family (3:14), and "members" of the same household (3:6; 10:21). The Bible does not advocate a hermit-like lifestyle for the Christian; rather, we are told to challenge, edify and encourage one another toward love and good works.

How can we best accomplish this task? We can fulfill this through faithful and involved church attendance. Verse 25 commands faithfulness to a local church. Your attendance is needed not just to feed your spirit but also to feed others! Your presence there is needed to encourage fellow believers.

Our Great Expectation (v. 25)

Verse 25 ends with the phrase "and so much the more as you see the Day approaching." The closer we get to His coming, the more we ought to gather together for worship. We are called to faithfulness by the truth of His second coming. As the church meets together, the members should anticipate, contemplate and celebrate the fact that Jesus is coming.

CONCLUSION

We have been called to enter in, hold fast, draw near, and come together. The church needs a fresh commitment of faithfulness to Christ today. Determine today to look forward in anticipation to His coming and encourage one another in the faith.

14

Do You Walk With Him or on Him?

For if we sin willfully after we have received the knowledge of the truth, there no longer remains a sacrifice for sins, but a certain fearful expectation of judgment, and fiery indignation which will devour the adversaries. Anyone who has rejected Moses' law dies without mercy on the testimony of two or three witnesses. Of how much worse punishment, do you suppose, will he be thought worthy who has trampled the Son of God underfoot, counted the blood of the covenant by which he was sanctified a common thing, and insulted the Spirit of grace? For we know Him who said, "Vengeance is Mine; I will repay," says the Lord. And again, "The Lord will judge His people." It is a fearful thing to fall into the hands of the living God. But recall the former days in which, after you were illuminated, you endured a great struggle with sufferings: partly while you were made a spectacle both by reproaches and tribulations, and partly while you became companions of those who were so treated; for you had compassion on me in my chains, and joyfully accepted the plundering of your goods, knowing that you have a better and an enduring possession for your-selves in heaven. Therefore do not cast away your con-fidence, which has great reward. For you have need of endurance, so that after you have done the will of God, you may receive the promise: "For yet a little while, and He who is coming will come and will not tarry. Now the just shall live by faith; but if anyone draws back, My soul has no pleasure in him." But we are not of those who draw back to perdition, but of those who believe to the saving of the soul (Hebrews 10:26-39).

INTRODUCTION

Faith, hope and love are the marks that should characterize our lives and our worship. To retreat from faith to works, from hope to temporal sight, and from love to law is a great tragedy. This retreat could be a sign of an unregenerate heart. This warning is the fourth of five warnings in the Book of Hebrews. I am convinced this warning has to do with the unsaved person.

The author of Hebrews was concerned about those who had received a "knowledge of the truth" (v. 26) but had rejected Christ. They had no assurance of faith, and no confession of hope. They lacked a "sincere heart" (v. 22, *NIV*) and continued to practice sin.

On the other hand, there were those who had endured all manner of difficulty and kept the faith. Some were walking *with* Jesus while others walked *on* Him. Look carefully at the two groups.

Those Who Walk on Him (10:26-31)

In verse 25, we observe that some people had quit fellowshipping with the church. They had deserted the faith, and had become moral apostates. They were not occasional sinners who were sorry for their sin. Their lives were a testimony that they had deserted Christ and the church. The truth is that they were never saved. They were like seed that fell on stony ground and showed growth, but they died when the heat of difficulty came because they had no spiritual roots. Look at the marks of these apostates.

The apostates rejected the Word of God (v. 28). This verse describes deliberate, high-handed sin in the face of knowledge. A person sins directly against the truth when a decision is made to practice sin.

A sinning lifestyle is a rejection of Calvary! The phrase "there no longer remains a sacrifice for sins" (v. 26) indicates that by living in constant sin, the sinner has repudiated the power of the Cross. The death of Jesus, when received by faith, breaks the power of sin. The believer can then live free from the shackles of sin. To live in open rebellion to truth is an indication of rejection of faith.

Those who rejected the old covenant died a physical death. But those who reject the sacrifice of Christ die eternally.

The apostates disdained the Son of God (v. 29). To reject the gospel is to "[have] trampled the Son of God underfoot" (v. 29). The author chose a poignant and powerful phrase to emphasize the awfulness of

Hebrews: Finding the Better Way

this treatment. When Jesus walked on earth, He used the word *trample* to describe what was done to salt that had become useless (Matthew 5:13). It was also used to describe what swine would do if you cast pearls in front of them (7:6). The author of Hebrews is saying that those who reject the gift of God treat Christ as though He is useless and without any value.

The apostates insulted the Spirit of God (Hebrews 10:29). Another word for *insulted* is "outraged." The translation seems to indicate this is the worst kind of indecent insult. God in His grace convicts the sinner. By rejecting Him, they insult the Spirit of the living God.

The apostates face the judgment of God (vv. 27, 29-31). The words of this passage have a clear warning: the judgment upon those who reject Christ is certain, terrifying and burning vengeance.

The Lord will punish the sinner and chasten the believer. But in this passage, the terrifying truth is that these lost people were attending a church. It is clear that some people may indeed know truth, but not personally know Christ. They may understand how the blood covenant with God works, but never enter into it. By choosing sin and walking away from Christ, they fly in the face of heaven and face an eternity in hell.

Just as ridiculous as it is to make a pet out of a deadly snake that has slithered into your nursery and injured your baby, so it is unreasonable for those who are saved to make a pet out of sin. That sin killed our Savior and continues to destroy the souls of men.

126

Those Who Walk With Him (10:32-39)

The writer of Hebrews plainly declares that those who are truly saved will not "cast away" their confidence (v. 35), and will not "draw back to perdition" (v. 39). What are the marks of those who truly walk with Jesus?

They are people of patience (vv. 32-34). One of the key truths about those who receive salvation is that they can endure. When first saved, the Hebrew believers had suffered. The word *struggle* (v. 32)—or "fight" (KJV), "conflict" (*NASB*)—come from the Greek word *athlesis*, from which our English word *athlete* also comes. It is a picture of someone who is willing to suffer as the price of victory. Those who are athletes know the pain of practice and the pain of competition.

These early believers also patiently endured public shame for their faith, both personally and corporately. They shared in the shame their fellow believers endured.

During the Holocaust in World War II when 6 million Jews were murdered, almost as many Christians also died. They gave their lives because they were willing to share the shame.

Also, these people had endured the loss of personal possessions. Their response to this loss was joy! When our property on this earth is stolen or broken, it should only make us thankful for our better possessions in glory.

They are people of promise (vv. 35-37). When the dust settles on all the trials of this life, we shall receive the promise of a better life. Our Lord is coming. The text says "yet a little while" (v. 37), for it won't be long until our days here on earth will end at the coming of Christ.

Until that day, we will hold on to our confidence and live by faith (v. 38). Our faith in Christ that saved us from sin will preserve us through difficulty. Walking with Jesus will take us to the mountaintop of joy and to the valley of service. There will often be a cross to bear, but one day we will wear a crown.

CONCLUSION

Do you walk with Jesus or trample Him under your feet of unbelief and rebellion? To depend on your own works is an insult to grace. To live in open sin when you know Christ died for those sins is an affront to Calvary.

Don't walk away from Christ, the loving appeal of the Father, and the pleadings of the Holy Spirit. Trust Him with your life today.

15

The Life of Faith

"Now the just shall live by faith; but if anyone draws back, My soul has no pleasure in him." But we are not of those who draw back to perdition, but of those who believe to the saving of the soul. Now faith is the substance of things hoped for, the evidence of things not seen. For by it the elders obtained a good testimony. By faith we understand that the worlds were framed by the word of God, so that the things which are seen were not made of things which are visible (Hebrews 10:38—11:3).

INTRODUCTION

The Lord Jesus Christ is superior to anyone or anything in the Old Testament. He is the fulfillment of all the rituals, symbols and prophecies found there. The passage in Hebrews 10:37, 38 is a quote of Habakkuk 2:3, 4: "For the vision is yet for an appointed time; but at the end it will speak, and it will not lie. Though it tarries, wait for it; because it will surely come, it will not tarry. Behold the proud, his soul is not upright in him; but the just shall live by his faith."

This prophecy strongly declares, "The just shall live by faith," which is later quoted in Romans 1:17 and Galatians 3:11. It is our faith in the superior worth and work of Christ that saves. To our comfort, not only does faith save—it also sustains.

Hebrews 11 first lays the foundation of faith and then gives illustrations of that faith. This chapter translates principles into practice. We find recorded in the pages of this letter to the Hebrews the great "honor roll" of the Old Testament. Those listed here are honored not for their works, but for their faith. This great galaxy of spiritual stars stands as an example of daring individuals of true faith lived out in life. God's hall of fame is filled with those who by faith performed their duty, faced their trials and received their blessings.

We should live our lives in the same superior way. We are to live by faith because without it, we cannot please God (v. 6).

The Definition of Faith (10:37-39)

What is *faith*? Faith is believing and trusting. Everyone has faith in something. The humanist has faith in himself and humanity. The materialist has faith in his possessions. Even the simple acts of life require faith.

Faith is only as valid as the object in which it is placed. Christian faith is believing in and acting upon the Word of God. Faith is the ear and eye of the soul. Just as the physical ear picks up sound waves, so the soul hears and sees the Word of God.

Faith is the hand of the soul that reaches out to lay hold on God's Word.

Several years ago, I took my family to an amusement park. Like most parks of this nature, the headlining attractions were gigantic, fearsome roller coasters! I could not convince some members of my family to ride the biggest roller coaster. It obviously could be safely ridden, as was clearly seen by the scores of people who came out of the exits every 40 seconds, laughing. Yet, my family members refused to ride it.

This is exactly what happened to the recipients of the letter to the Hebrews. They had heard and seen, but they feared an all-out abandonment of their former life for what they saw to be a risky ride with Jesus.

Some people today have an intellectual belief in Jesus, but they refuse to trust Him with the rest of themselves. Faith is more than simply knowing what God has said; faith is responding positively to what He has said. The Book of Hebrews declares God's last word to be Jesus.

The Dimensions of Faith (11:1)

Here we are given the two dimensions of faith: faith to face the future, and faith to live in the present.

Faith to look ahead. "Faith is the substance" (v. 1). The word *substance* comes from the Greek word *hupostasis,* which means "to place beneath" or "that which stands under." It can mean a foundation or a strong assurance.

These definitions tell us that our faith in the future is based on what God has promised. Our faith is the title deed to all of God's promises. Many of God's promised blessings are not yet mine. I do not have my resurrection body, my mansion in glory, nor the blessing of being like Him. I have, however, His promise in writing. When faith lays hold of a promise, it becomes yours before you have it.

Faith to look beyond. Faith is called "the evidence of things not seen" (v. 1). The word *evidence* translates from the Greek word *elengchos,* which is translated as "conviction" in other places (John 8:46; 16:8).

The true believer is convinced that there is an unseen world more real than the temporal world. Christians believe in those things that the physical eye cannot see.

I haven't seen Jesus, yet I believe. First Peter 1:6-8 teaches us that it is love for the unseen Jesus in the midst of trials that is the proof of faith.

> In this you greatly rejoice, though now for a little while, if need be, you have been grieved by various trials, that the genuineness of your faith, being much more precious than gold that perishes, though it is tested by fire, may be found to praise, honor, and glory at the revelation of Jesus Christ, whom having not seen you love. Though now you do not see Him, yet believing, you rejoice with joy inexpressible and full of glory.

I haven't seen the victory, yet I believe it has been won. When I see the overwhelming wickedness of our day, and the seeming triumphs of Satan, I remember Hebrews 2:8, "we do not yet see all things put under Him." However, by faith we know all things are under Him.

These two dimensions of faith make life in a sin-cursed world tolerable. No matter how difficult the present circumstances seem, the faithful believer has invisible resources. Furthermore, the future is as bright as God's promises.

The Daring of Faith (11:2)

The Old Testament characters heralded in Hebrews were people of faith. They had received the witness of God and acted on that witness.

The words *good report* (KJV) also have been translated "witness." Some believe this means that God saw their faith and approved it. However, I am convinced that it carries a deeper meaning. The Old Testament saints looked ahead of their situation, beyond their circumstances, and received the witness of heaven. Having received the witness of heaven, they acted on that witness and became part of the evidence of faith.

The examples abound:

- Abel looked ahead and saw the Lamb of God.

- Noah saw the flood and God's way of safety.

- Abraham saw Calvary and the Resurrection in the offering of Isaac.

- Moses saw that the riches of Christ were greater than the wealth of this world.

Faith receives the witness of God as final and acts on that word, regardless of human conditions or outward circumstances.

The Dynamics of Faith (11:3)

How can we put this life of faith into practice? In verse 3, we are reminded of the power of God's Word. It was God's Word that set in motion the ages of history. God created this world and its subsequent history out of nothing!

If God could call this world out of nothing, then by faith I believe He can call something out of nothing even today. Once we have a word from God's Word, we can trust Him to take care of what He has shown us. Our job is to act on that word. Faith calls it done, simply because God has said it.

Here we find that the translation of *word* is not the usual *logos*. It is *rhema*, meaning "spoken word." It is not enough to look up a verse and then claim it. That word must be spoken to your spirit by God's Spirit. The creative word of power must be spoken to you. When God speaks a word to your spirit from the Scriptures, call it done in Jesus' name!

Here are the steps for moving into a life of faith:

- The word of faith must be heard (Romans 10).

- The word of faith must be received and believed.

- The word of faith must be confessed.
- The word of faith must be acted upon.

CONCLUSION

God does not want you in the dark about your future. He will give you a word if you will read His written Word and listen to the Holy Spirit. Once you have a clear word from God, then confess it to others, and act upon it.

This is how you discover God's will in any matter. God will give you a clear word from the Scripture if you will trust Him. This is also how someone is saved. God speaks the word of salvation. You believe it, confess it, and act upon it. Faith saves us and sustains us.

16

The Word of His Power

By faith we understand that the worlds were framed by the word of God, so that the things which are seen were not made of things which are visible (Hebrews 11:3).

INTRODUCTION

Faith is believing and acting on God's Word. Faith is only as valid as the object in which it is placed. Our Christian faith is valid because it is based on the Word of God. As we discussed in the previous chapter, there are two words that are translated *word* in the New Testament—*logos* and *rhema*. According to author Ralph Speas, these words can be set alongside each other as follows:

LOGOS	RHEMA
Word	Expressed or spoken word
Truth	Specific truth
Message	Personal message
Scripture	Quickening scripture
Results in knowledge, wisdom and understanding	Results in faith, spirit and life

Logos

The Lord Jesus himself illustrates this truth. In John
1:1, 14, we discover that Jesus was and is the *Logos*
or "Word of God." In verse 14 we are told that the
Logos became flesh. Jesus was the Word and became
the expressed word. Jesus, who is truth, became specific truth. Jesus came as God's personal message to
us. Hebrews 1:2, 3 indicates that God spoke His final
word to man in Jesus. Jesus was the expression of
the reality of God's character. Also it is said that Jesus
upholds all things by the *rhema* of His power.

Faith is not blind reliance on God's Word; it is a
persuasion of its veracity, wisdom and power. As
Arthur Pink once said, "Christians are the wisest of
earth's inhabitants." The fools on earth are those who
are "slow of heart" to believe God (Luke 24:25).

According to our text, the Creation came into existence through the "word of God" (Hebrews 11:3).
God spoke and the word of His power brought the
world and all of its ages into being with exactness
and precision. God spoke and the galaxies exploded
in radiance and beauty, and the solar system whirled
into order! At His voice, the earth roared to life, with
the mountains rising in stately majesty. At His word,
the lions roared, the birds sang, the trees waved their
branches toward heaven. God spoke and the world
burst forth in glorious color and sound.

God's word expressed gave life and glory to the
created order. God spoke and man came forth from
the original womb, the hollow of God's hand. God

taught man to do something no other creature can do, and that is speak with words.

Rhema

What is the significance of this? When God's word (*logos*) becomes a personal word (*rhema*) to your spirit, it comes with the same power that brought the world into being!

This is the same truth found in Romans 10:8-17. The word of God saves when it is received, believed and confessed. "Faith comes by hearing, and hearing by the word [*rhema*] of God" (v. 17).

Simply reading the Bible will not produce faith. Instead, allowing the truth to become personal is the key. It is one thing to know the Bible teaches that Jesus will save. It is quite another thing to receive and confess that truth personally.

The *rhema* is a word of His power. It is the word that sustains the spirit. In Matthew 4:4, Jesus said to Satan, "Man shall not live by bread alone, but by every word [*rhema*] that proceeds from the mouth of God." In order for the Bible to feed you, it must become *rhema*. To study just for the sake of studying, rather than for finding a message for life, is to fill your head but starve your spirit!

Look at Luke 24:13-32 as an illustration of this truth. Two disciples grieving over the death of Jesus were walking to Emmaus from Jerusalem. The risen Jesus drew near, but they did not recognize Him. Jesus rebuked them for their unbelief. These men knew the Old Testament Scriptures. They knew the *logos* of God. Yet that word had not come alive by faith. Jesus then took the *logos* and made *rhema* out of it. Notice their comment in verses 31 and 32: "Then their eyes were opened and they knew Him; and He vanished from their sight. And they said to one another, 'Did not our heart burn within us while He talked with us on the road, and while He opened the Scriptures to us?'" A fire burned in their hearts as Jesus opened the Scriptures!

When you see Jesus and hear His voice speaking to your need, rebuking your sin, instructing you in your trial and encouraging you in your distress—that is *rhema*.

Furthermore, the *rhema* of God is our weapon. In Ephesians 6:17 it is the *rhema* of God that is called "the sword of the Spirit." When we confess the Word out loud in the face of the Enemy, the Word is the formidable weapon we need.

The *rhema* is also the secret to success in Christian work. In Luke 5:1-11 we see this beautifully portrayed. Jesus borrowed Simon's boat as a pulpit in order to speak to the crowds on the lakeside. As they pulled away from the shore, Jesus illustrated the power and authority of His word, by telling Simon to put down the fishing net. Simon was reluctant, but said, "Nevertheless at Your word [*rhema*] I will let down the net" (v. 5). Peter and his shipmates were astonished at the huge catch that resulted! It was the word of His power that brought the fish in. In that same passage, Jesus said to them, "Do not be afraid. From now on you will catch men" (v. 10). How do we reach people? We fish where He says to fish, and when He says to fish! He speaks with a word of power.

CONCLUSION

"'The word is near you, in your mouth and in your heart' (that is, the word of faith which we preach)" (Romans 10:8). The great men of faith in Hebrews 11 received and confessed the Word of God. They lived by the word of His power.

Can you receive God's Word personally? Can the *logos* become *rhema* in your heart? If you are not saved, then act today on the Word of salvation.

If you are a believer, it should be the deepest desire of your heart to know what Jesus is saying to you. Your life ought to be a life of faith. Is there evidence of the word of His power in your life? In John 15:7, Jesus said, "If you abide in Me, and My words abide in you, you will ask what you desire, and it shall be done for you."

Knowing His heart is not simply claiming a verse of Scripture. God's Word must live in you as *rhema*, the word of His power.

17

The Life That Pleases God

By faith Abel offered to God a more excellent sacrifice than Cain, through which he obtained witness that he was righteous, God testifying of his gifts; and through it he being dead still speaks. By faith Enoch was taken away so that he did not see death, "and was not found, because God had taken him"; for before he was taken he had this testimony, that he pleased God. But without faith it is impossible to please Him, for he who comes to God must believe that He is, and that He is a rewarder of those who diligently seek Him. By faith Noah, being divinely warned of things not yet seen, moved with godly fear, prepared an ark for the saving of his household, by which he condemned the world and became heir of the righteousness which is according to faith (Hebrews 11:4-7).

INTRODUCTION

Besides the title "God's Hall of Fame," this section of Hebrews has been called the "Westminster Abbey of the Bible" and the "Roll Call of Faith." The writer of Hebrews uses the Old Testament to demonstrate to his readers that God's way has always been the way of faith.

Faith looks beyond to an invisible realm through the Word of God. Faith acts on the basis of what God says. In these verses, three characters illustrate the kind of life that pleases God.

Abel: The Approach of Faith (11:4)

Abel was the second-born son of Adam and Eve, the brother of Cain. Abel's faith answers a basic question about worship: How does a person approach God?

Notice what Abel offered. Abel came with a valuable offering, the firstling of his flock. More significant than its value is the nature of the offering. Abel came with an offering of blood "in the process of time" (Genesis 4:3)—or according to the Hebrew, "at the end of days," which we take to mean on the Sabbath (JFB Commentary).

Abel's offering of a blood sacrifice displayed that he recognized his sinful nature. Knowing he was deserving of death, Abel offered a substitute for his sin. By faith, Abel knew that man needed an innocent substitute to atone for sin. Abel came with a sincere heart and offered the more excellent sacrifice—looking ahead to Calvary where better blood would be shed for the sins of the world, the blood of Christ (Hebrews 12:24).

Notice what Abel obtained. Abel obtained heaven's witness that he was righteous. Abel was saved by his faith. However, faith did not eliminate his problems. Abel was hated by his brother, Cain, who later murdered him. Cain is an example of all those who reject the way of faith. He was too proud to offer a blood sacrifice, yet his wicked heart did not hesitate to shed his own brother's blood. Abel's life teaches us all that the only way a sinner can approach God is by faith in the blood of Jesus Christ.

Enoch: The Attitude of Faith (11:5)

Enoch was a mysterious character. He was the first man recorded in the Bible to enter heaven without dying. Genesis 5:21-24 records the unusual testimony of Enoch. The Scripture says, "Enoch walked with God" (v. 22). Enoch's life teaches us how to live the faith life.

To walk with God implies compatibility. Amos 3:3 asks, "Can two walk together, unless they are agreed?" The answer is no. To walk with God implies agreement. Enoch lived his life in harmony with God.

To walk with God also implies confession of sin. The word *confess* means "to agree with God." In order for Enoch to walk with God, he agreed with God that he had sin in his life, but he lived in a repentant spirit. You can just imagine Enoch coming before God and saying, "Dear Lord, I can't walk with You and carry this sin burden; help me to be rid of it."

To walk with God leads to blessed communion. If we walk with Him, we are in fellowship with Him. There will be a genuine love, devotion and affection toward God.

Did Enoch see God physically on earth? The answer is no. He looked beyond this world and by faith took hold of the hand of the invisible God to walk with

Him. Enoch was raptured to heaven without dying. A little girl in a Sunday school once described Enoch's home-going this way: "One day the fellowship was so sweet that God said to Enoch, "It is late and we're nearer My house than yours; come on home with Me."

Our life of faith ought to be a walk with God until, at the hour of death or at the sound of the trumpet, we are called home to be with Him.

Noah: The Activity of Faith (11:7)

Noah teaches us that "faith without works is dead" (James 2:20). By faith Noah worked, not to be saved, but because he was saved.

Noah looked ahead and beyond, and received a word from God. God's word was a warning and a command. Noah was to build a large ship. He was told exactly how to build a vessel where there had never been a drop of rain, let alone a flood.

Noah worked by faith. The only evidence he had for the coming disaster was the word from God. Noah labored for 120 years without regard for what people thought. He worked and preached without a convert. Noah held to the word of God.

Noah was moved with fear and reverence. When the ark was finished, Noah's family was saved, but the world was condemned.

We learn from Noah that faith moves at God's word. Dr. Percy Ray was a church planter for many years with the Southern Baptist Home Mission Board. Back in the late 1940s, God told him to build a large assembly hall where Christians could gather. God told him to stand in the middle of the land in Myrtle, Mississippi, and start digging the footing for a 2,000-seat assembly hall. So he went out there and started digging, and folks laughed at him. However, one day a man came along and gave Dr. Ray a check to pay for the entire shell of the building. This wealthy man was praying in Memphis, and God told him to ride down into northern Mississippi where he would find a preacher digging a footing for a building, and he was to give that man a large amount of money! Camp Zion stands today as one of the great Christian assembly halls in America. Dr. Ray obeyed God, and the blessing came.

CONCLUSION

Hebrews 11:6 says, "Without faith it is impossible to please [God]." A person can do nothing to gain the favor of God, except to trust Him. Abel teaches us that the only way a sinner can approach God is by faith in the blood of Jesus Christ. Enoch teaches us how to please God in our daily walk. Noah teaches us the importance of obeying God in the area of works.

Faith can carry us through the treachery of others, and can even help us overcome death. Faith carries us through catastrophe, even worldwide chaos.

To come to God you must "believe that He is, and that He is a rewarder of those who diligently seek Him" (v. 6). If we are to know God, we must accept His existence and believe in His generosity. Have you sought Him? Will you cast your cares on Him today?

18

The Tests of Faith

By faith Abraham obeyed when he was called to go out to the place which he would receive as an inheritance. And he went out, not knowing where he was going. By faith he dwelt in the land of promise as in a foreign country, dwelling in tents with Isaac and Jacob, the heirs with him of the same promise; for he waited for the city which has foundations, whose builder and maker is God. By faith Sarah herself also received strength to conceive seed, and she bore a child when she was past the age, because she judged Him faithful who had promised. Therefore from one man, and him as good as dead, were born as many as the stars of the sky in multitude—innumerable as the sand which is by the seashore. These all died in faith, not having received the promises, but having seen them afar off were assured of them, embraced them and confessed that they were strangers and pilgrims on the earth. For those who say such things declare plainly that they seek a homeland. And truly if they had called to mind that country from which they had come out, they would have had opportunity to return. But now they desire a better, that is, a heavenly country. Therefore God is not ashamed to be called their God, for He has prepared a city for them. By faith Abraham, when he was tested, offered up Isaac, and he who had received the promises offered up his only begotten son, of whom it was said, "In Isaac your seed shall be called," concluding that God was able to raise him up, even from the dead, from which he also received him in a figurative sense (Hebrews 11:8-19).

INTRODUCTION

Abraham is the greatest example of faith in the Old Testament. Some interesting truths about Abraham are worth studying.

Abraham is the progenitor of the physical seed through which God would bless the world. After the destruction of the Tower of Babel and the scattering of humanity, God chose to deal with the world through the seed of Abraham. "Now the Lord had said to Abram: 'Get out of your country, from your family and from your father's house, to a land that I will show you. I will make you a great nation; I will bless you and make your name great; and you shall be a blessing' " (Genesis 12:1, 2).

Abraham is the patriarch of all who believe. Romans 4:11 says of Abraham, "that he might be the father of all those who believe." This is a reference to the fact that Abraham "believed in the Lord, and He accounted it to him for righteousness" (Genesis 15:6). Abraham is the father of all who believe.

Abraham sets the pattern for the faith life. "Therefore He who supplies the Spirit to you and works miracles among you, does He do it by the works of the law, or by the hearing of faith?—just as Abraham 'believed God, and it was accounted to him for righteousness.' Therefore know that only those who are of faith are sons of Abraham" (Galatians 3:5-7). Verse 29 declares that Abraham's family is related to all believers: "And if you are Christ's, then you are Abraham's seed, and heirs according to the promise."

Furthermore, John 8:39-44 declares the true children of Abraham are those who follow the faith-filled lifestyle of Abraham:

They answered and said to Him, "Abraham is our father." Jesus said to them, "If you were Abraham's children, you would do the works of Abraham. But now you seek to kill Me, a Man who has told you the truth which I heard from God. Abraham did not do this. You do the deeds of your father." Then they said to Him, "We were not born of fornication; we have one Father—God." Jesus said to them, "If God were your Father, you would love Me, for I proceeded forth and came from God; nor have I come of Myself, but He sent Me. Why do you not understand My speech? Because you are not able to listen to My word. You are of your father the devil, and the desires of your father you want to do. He was a murderer from the beginning, and does not stand in the truth, because there is no truth in him. When he speaks a lie, he speaks from his own resources, for he is a liar and the father of it.

So great was this patriarch's faith that God called him friend!

"But you, Israel, are My servant, Jacob whom I have chosen, the descendants of Abraham My friend" (Isaiah 41:8).

And the Scripture was fulfilled which says, "Abraham believed God, and it was accounted to him for righteousness." And he was called the friend of God (James 2:23).

We can learn from the faith of Abraham. Three great tests were placed against Abraham's faith. Every test centered on the promises God had made to Abraham, and Abraham passed all three tests.

The Tests of Worldliness (11:8-10, 13-16)

Abraham, a true man of faith, could never be at home in this world. Abraham was a wealthy citizen of Ur of the Chaldeans. He had a house, property and a family. He lived among a pagan people who worshiped the moon, but in His sovereign grace God called Abraham for His purposes. Abraham caught a vision of a heavenly city and could never be at home again in this world.

And Joshua said to all the people, "Thus says the Lord God of Israel: 'Your fathers, including Terah, the father of Abraham and the father of Nahor, dwelt on the other side of the River in old times; and they served other gods. Then I took your father Abraham from the other side of the River, led him throughout all the land of Canaan, and multiplied his descendants and gave him Isaac' " (Joshua 24:2, 3).

"Listen to Me, you who follow after righteousness, you who seek the Lord: look to the rock from which you were hewn, and to the hole of the pit from which you were dug. Look to Abraham your father, and to Sarah who bore you; for I called him alone, and blessed him and increased him" (Isaiah 51:1, 2).

Abraham was called to separate from his country, his family, and his father's house. He was told to leave Ur (modern-day Iraq).

It is easy to forget this, but God did not give Abraham a map of the Middle East, point to a location and say, "Here is where you are going, Abraham." Abraham obeyed and left, without knowing his destination. The scripture says, "For he waited for the city which has foundations, whose builder and maker is God" (Hebrews 11:10).

Abraham learned that *a* city won't do when you have caught a glimpse of *the* City. Bible scholar John Phillips, commenting on the pilgrim character of the people, shares this observation. The symbols of the patriarch were a tent and an altar. The tent symbolized a relationship with the world. The great patriarchs of the faith were temporary citizens of this world—just passing through. The symbol of the altar illustrated their relationship to God. Hebrews 11:13-16 declares that what Abraham longed for was also the desire of all the patriarchs.

Furthermore, the City of God ought to be the desire of all God's faithful today. Paul declared in Philippians 3:20, "For our citizenship is in heaven, from which we also eagerly wait for the Savior, the Lord Jesus Christ."

When you view Abraham and those who followed his example, you note that our faith is a pilgrim's faith. As a young boy I learned a song that said:

> I am a stranger here
> Within a foreign land.
> My home is far away
> Upon a Golden Strand.[1]

Later in the country churches where I served, I learned this song:

> This world is not my home,
> I'm only passing through.
> My treasures are laid up,
> Somewhere beyond the blue.
> The angels beckon me,
> From heaven's open door,
> And I can't feel at home,
> In this world anymore.[2]

Our faith is not only a pilgrim faith—it is also a *performing* faith. Abraham did exactly what God called him to do (Hebrews 11:8). Then faith becomes a *preserving* faith (vv. 9, 10, 13-16). Both Abraham

[1] From hymn "The King's Business," Flora and E.T. Cassel.
[2] From song "I Can't Feel at Home in this World," copyright 1951.

and his faithful descendants lived on the promises of God. They saw the promises of God, welcomed them and confessed them continually (v. 13).

John Wesley once said, "Anything that cools my love for Jesus is worldliness." Are you more comfortable here than you would be in heaven? Would the coming of Jesus interrupt all your plans? The true believer cannot become comfortable in this world.

The Test of Weakness (11:11, 12)

Abraham and Sarah had been promised a descendant. But they had passed the age of child bearing. "Then Abraham fell on his face and laughed, and said in his heart, 'Shall a child be born to a man who is one hundred years old? And shall Sarah, who is ninety years old, bear a child?'" (Genesis 17:17).

Furthermore, Sarah was barren. "But Sarai was barren; she had no child" (11:30).

Humanly speaking, we would look at this as an impossible situation. Yet, God had promised. Abraham and Sarah were given the strength of young people for the purpose of bringing Isaac into the world. The key is in Hebrews 11:11: "She judged Him faithful who had promised." Romans 4:16-22 sheds even more light on the truth:

> Therefore it is of faith that it might be according to grace, so that the promise might be sure to all the seed, not only to those who are of the law, but also to those who are of the faith of Abraham, who is the father of

us all (as it is written, "I have made you a father of many nations") in the presence of Him whom he believed—God, who gives life to the dead and calls those things which do not exist as though they did; who, contrary to hope, in hope believed, so that he became the father of many nations, according to what was spoken, "So shall your descendants be." And not being weak in faith, he did not consider his own body, already dead (since he was about a hundred years old), and the deadness of Sarah's womb. He did not waver at the promise of God through unbelief, but was strengthened in faith, giving glory to God, and being fully convinced that what He had promised He was also able to perform.

Think of the glory of their testimony! No doubt, old Abraham looked at Sarah and saw instead of a 90-year-old wife, his youthful bride. I believe that even as Sarah began to show the physical signs of her pregnancy, old Abraham ran all over the camp shouting, "Glory to God!" No wonder Sarah named that little boy *Isaac*, which means "laughter."

From this story, we learn that God is not limited by human weaknesses. In a former church I pastored, a sweet young couple was burdened because they could not have children. They had one adopted daughter, but the young wife came forward during a service and asked the church to pray that God would allow them to have another child. She said that God had given her a word that they would receive another child. Of course, she meant to ask the church to pray for another adoption to go through. A year later this dear lady gave birth to a child! The doctors didn't understand how because their examinations concluded that there was no way her womb could have accomplished this!

Faith can overcome human weakness. This also applies to God's work. When we feel inadequate or unable, God can move through the weakness. Faith does not waver in the face of human shortcomings and infirmities.

The Test of Willingness (11:17-19)

Abraham was first tested in the areas of mental reasoning and physical weakness.

Next he was tested in his heart and soul. Would he surrender to God the most precious thing in his life? Genesis 22 records this heart-moving event when Abraham was asked to sacrifice his miracle child to God as an offering.

I think it is clear from the story that Abraham had totally purposed in his heart to offer Isaac, but he was also just as convinced that God would immediately raise Isaac from the dead. Look at Genesis 22:5, "And Abraham said to his young men, 'Stay here with the donkey; the lad and I will go yonder and worship, and we will come back to you.'"

In Hebrews 11:18, 19, we find that Abraham believed the promise God had made for a great nation to come from Isaac. He knew God could raise Isaac from the ashes to keep His word.

In his heart, no doubt Abraham had already put Isaac to death. Isaac serves as a type of Christ. He carried the wood on his back up Mount Moriah. Abraham looked ahead to Calvary and the empty tomb from the slopes of Moriah.

Abraham died to self and to all his ambition on that day. He staked his whole life and future on the Word of God. Faith is willing to surrender all to Jesus.

CONCLUSION

How does your own faith measure up in these tests? What pull does the world and what it offers have on you? Do you make excuses through your weaknesses and inabilities? Would you give up the dearest thing or person in your life if He asked you to?

Our Lord Jesus surrendered it all for us. When the cross was put on His back, and He journeyed up the mountain of Calvary, there was no reprieve. The knife of sacrifice and fire of judgment fell on Him. It is faith in Him that begins the journey to the heavenly city.

19

The Victory of Faith

By faith Isaac blessed Jacob and Esau concerning things to come. By faith Jacob, when he was dying, blessed each of the sons of Joseph, and worshiped, leaning on the top of his staff. By faith Joseph, when he was dying, made mention of the departure of the children of Israel, and gave instructions concerning his bones (Hebrews 11:20-22).

INTRODUCTION

It is at the end of life that faith's victory is seen most clearly. The dying utterances of the three Old Testament patriarchs demonstrate that victory. Hebrews 11:13-16 declared the testimony of all of the patriarchs. These faithful people climbed the mountains of life's difficulties and with keen spiritual vision glanced over into the glorious future of all who believe. The promises of God were welcomed from a distance; they were hailed with delight and embraced. Death was no terror to them in old age—they had looked ahead. They all died giving a blessing, and though they never saw the promises made to them come in fullness, they died believing.

How will you face the end of your life? You can know victory at the end of life's road. Isaac, Jacob and Joseph each illustrate one aspect of faith's victory.

Isaac: Victory Over the Flesh (v. 20)

The mark of Isaac's life was submissiveness. He submitted when Abraham took him to Mount Moriah. He was submissive in the selection of his wife, Rebekah (see Genesis 24). He was submissive and full of peace as he watched the Philistines capture one water well after another he had dug with his own hands. As they laid claim to one, Isaac would just dig another.

However, this phlegmatic man had a fleshly weakness. Though God had told Isaac and his wife, Rebekah, that Jacob was the chosen son, Isaac showed more favor to the athletic outdoorsman son, Esau, than to the crafty Jacob. The flesh was Isaac's weakness.

The worst problem was Isaac's appetite for meat (Genesis 25:28; 27:3-5). Because of the flesh, Isaac was willing to change the decree of God. Knowing her husband's weaknesses, Rebekah helped put together a scheme to get the fatherly blessing placed on Jacob instead of Esau. She put animal skins on Jacob's hands and the smooth part of his neck and fixed savory food for him to present to his father. The half-blind Isaac gave the blessing to Jacob.

Where does faith enter into this scheme? Faith is clearly seen when Isaac, knowing he had been deceived, refuses to reverse the decree and transfer the blessing to Esau (Genesis 27:30-41). Hebrews 12:16, 17 to grant him the blessing instead, but Isaac would not repent of the blessing. In the end, Isaac believed and held to the Word of God. Genesis 27 records the supreme blessing on Jacob and the secondary blessing of Esau.

Faith acts on what God says, not on what the flesh sees. God's decree, not man's desire, must govern our lives. Isaac acted on the word of God.

Do fleshly appearances, affections and appetites govern your life? Faith can gain the victory over flesh.

Jacob: Victory Over the World (v. 21)

God appeared to Jacob five times. On every occasion the purpose was chastening and correction. On his deathbed, Jacob blessed Ephraim and Manasseh, the sons of his own son Joseph. Jacob finally had become Israel—he was now blessing the people of God.

The lost man dies not blessing but cursing, because he is leaving everything behind. Jacob had learned through experience that believers can never be at home in this world.

We note that in his final days, Jacob worshiped while leaning on a staff. What a contrast to his younger years when he wrestled with God. According to Genesis 32:24-30, the Lord touched Jacob's leg during that experience and knocked it out of joint.

Then Jacob was left alone; and a Man wrestled with him until the breaking of day. Now when He saw that He did not prevail against him, He touched the socket of his hip; and the socket of Jacob's hip was out of joint as He wrestled with him. And He said, "Let Me go, for the day breaks." But he said, "I will not let You go unless You bless me!" So He said to him, "What is your name?" He said, "Jacob." And He said, "Your name shall no longer be called Jacob, but Israel; for you have struggled with God and with men, and have prevailed." Then Jacob asked, saying, "Tell me Your name, I pray." And He said, "Why is it that you ask about My name?" And He blessed him there. So Jacob called the name of the place Peniel: "For I have seen God face to face, and my life is preserved."

For the rest of his life, Jacob halted or limped. That staff was a mark of glory for Jacob. Only when God chastened Jacob did he learn to lean on Jesus. Jacob worshiped the One who had brought him victory over the world.

Joseph: Victory Over the Devil (v. 22)

Joseph, in his dying requests, disdains the wealth of Egypt for the pleasures of Zion. Few men were more mistreated in all of the Old Testament than Joseph. He was sold into slavery, lied about, betrayed; but through it all, he remained faithful. Like Job of old, Joseph would not "charge God with wrong" (Job 1:22). God vindicated the faith of Joseph. Satan had no hold in the life of Joseph. Joseph's faith brought him through every circumstance.

Hebrews 11:22 speaks of Joseph's dying faith. His last word to his countrymen was, "As you go back to Canaan, carry up my bones." This request was to serve as a reminder to the nation that Egypt was not their home (Genesis 50:24-26). How strange that of all the events of Joseph's life, this event would be chosen to be listed in the "Hall of Fame."

The Holy Spirit could have chosen to mention Joseph's purity when he refused the advances of Potiphar's wife (Genesis 39). The Spirit could have chosen to extol his upright conduct while he was in jail, or when he interpreted Pharaoh's dream (Genesis 40). His faith could have been illustrated in the magnanimous way he forgave his brothers (Genesis 43—45). Rather, the Holy Spirit chose to refer to the dying utterance of Joseph. Joseph wanted to be buried in Israel. He could have had a pyramid or a fancy tomb, but all he wanted was a simple grave in his homeland.

Look closely at what faith saw. Joseph saw ahead to the wretched enslavement of his people. His bones would be a memorial. Those bones would say to the nation, writhing in agony under the rule of Pharaoh, "God will deliver you!"

We have a memorial we take part in today. We come to take Communion at the Lord's Table, and it reminds us that we have a future in the kingdom of heaven. Joseph's bones were a promise of home. The Lord's Supper is our promise of home.

CONCLUSION

We shall all come to the end of life. We can come to it in faith, shouting victory over the world, the flesh and the devil.

Faith is the victory!
Faith is the victory!
Oh, glorious victory
That overcomes the world." [1]

---

[1] From hymn "Faith Is the Victory," John H. Yates, 1891.

20

Faith for All of Life

By faith Moses, when he was born, was hidden three months by his parents, because they saw he was a beautiful child; and they were not afraid of the king's command. By faith Moses, when he became of age, refused to be called the son of Pharaoh's daughter, choosing rather to suffer affliction with the people of God than to enjoy the passing pleasures of sin, esteeming the reproach of Christ greater riches than the treasures in Egypt; for he looked to the reward. By faith he forsook Egypt, not fearing the wrath of the king; for he endured as seeing Him who is invisible. By faith he kept the Passover and the sprinkling of blood, lest he who destroyed the firstborn should touch them. By faith they passed through the Red Sea as by dry land, whereas the Egyptians, attempting to do so, were drowned (Hebrews 11:23-29).

INTRODUCTION

Next to Abraham, Moses was the most highly regarded ancestor of Israel. Our Lord Jesus said of the first five books of the Bible, "[Moses] wrote of me" (John 5:46, KJV).

Moses' life illustrates faith in action and serves as a model for all of us. The writer of Hebrews selects three primary events in the life of Moses to illustrate three marks of complete faith.

Parental Faith (11:23)

The first faith that operated in Moses' life was the faith of his parents, Amram and Jochebed. The account of Moses' birth and infancy is found in Exodus 2. Amram and Jochebed were two Jewish slaves who married during the oppression of Egyptian slavery. They were not notably different from others who were slaves, except for their faith.

Pharaoh ordered all Jewish male children to be cast into the Nile River. However, Amram and Jochebed hid Moses for three months. Finally, they made a small boat of bulrushes and set Moses adrift in the Nile. These two ordinary people believed in the sovereignty of God. They could no longer hide their baby, so they did the only thing they could do.

Imagine how their hearts ached when they looked at that beautiful little boy, knowing the sentence of death was upon him. I can hear Jochebed saying to Amram, "We can't let them kill our beautiful baby." They violated human authority because they believed in a higher authority, the authority of God.

Their faith acted rationally and carefully in preparing the little boat of bulrushes. The parents had their young daughter Miriam follow that boat. She was amazed to see it come to rest near where an Egyptian princess bathed. Pharaoh's daughter took the child as

166

her own, and thanks to quick thinking by Miriam, Jochebed became the baby's nurse in the palace of Pharaoh until he was 12 years of age.

We can see in this account the importance of faith in protecting our children. Parental faith was essential in saving an entire nation! What these simple people did for their own child would sway the future of a nation.

America needs to learn this! Parental faith can protect our children, and it may save our nation. The world and its modern pharaohs have no regard for babies. The abortion mills of America are killing our future. Parents are responsible, regardless of their circumstances, to rear their children to know the Lord.

Personal Faith (11:24-26)

The faith of godly parents can rear a child right, but it cannot carry the child through its lifetime. Parental faith can save a child from danger, but it cannot save a child from damnation. There comes a point where the child's personal faith must take over. Moses' parents had saved him from the world's dangers; but as he grew, his own faith had to deliver him from the world's allurements. Moses had to make his own decision.

Moses chose to refuse the throne of Egypt (v. 24). Moses was the son of Pharaoh's daughter. Moses was a man of social position and prominence. He was a prince of Egypt. Pharaoh's daughter had protected him, educated him and provided for him. Yet, he chose to say goodbye to what had been his home for 40 years.

167

Moses refused the temptations of Egypt (v. 25). The city of Pharaoh offered every possible temptation for a man of position. Moses could have had anything he wanted, yet he said no. He chose to be with God's people in affliction rather than have temporary pleasure. Moses knew that sin's pleasures are short-lived.

Moses refused the treasures of Egypt (v. 26). Moses chose God over wealth. He looked ahead and saw the freedom of his people, and chose God's riches.

Moses made a choice for a greater people, the people of God. He chose an eternal position over temporary pleasure. He chose the imperishable riches of Christ over the wealth of this world. Moses looked ahead and saw eternal glory! The tinsel and glitter of this world looked cheap and tawdry from that point onward.

It is easy to be discouraged as we face reproach here on earth, but there will be rejoicing in heaven. We may be cursed here, but there we will be crowned. George Beverly Shea's great song says it this way:

> I'd rather have Jesus than silver or gold,
> I'd rather be His than have riches untold;
> I'd rather have Jesus than houses or land,
> I'd rather be led by His nail pierced hand.

Practical Faith (11:27-29)

Personal faith becomes powerful faith when it acts on God's Word. Moses' faith demonstrated victory through three separate events.

Moses left Egypt (v. 27). In leaving Egypt, Moses demonstrated faith's victory over the world.

Moses kept the Passover (v. 28). In doing this, Moses demonstrated faith's victory over death. Moses rested under the blood of the Passover Lamb.

Moses led the children of Israel through the Red Sea (v. 29). Faith not only rests under the blood of the Passover Lamb, but it also walks through the impossibilities of life.

Faith must forsake the world, hide under the blood, and walk with God toward the promised land of abundant life.

CONCLUSION

We have seen what the faith of parents can do. We have seen the importance of personal faith and the choices it must make. We have seen faith practiced as it walks with God through the seas of difficulty.

What kept Moses going? Verse 27 says, "For he endured as seeing Him who is invisible." Have you seen the invisible with eyes of faith? Have you met Christ and surrendered all to Him?

As a child, Abraham Berringer came to the United States on the same ship that John Wesley had once traveled. Tragically, Abraham's parents died en route and the boy was reared as an orphan. When he grew up, he surrendered his life to missions. Berringer went to preach to the slaves on the island of St. Thomas. A law existed at the time that only a slave could teach a slave. So, Abraham Berringer wrote a letter requesting to become a slave so he could preach to the slaves. Later, the authorities gave him freedom to preach to any and all, regardless of color or social standing. Here was a man who, like Moses, put Christ first.

21
Faith for the Tough Times

By faith the walls of Jericho fell down after they were encircled for seven days. By faith the harlot Rahab did not perish with those who did not believe, when she had received the spies with peace. And what more shall I say? For the time would fail me to tell of Gideon and Barak and Samson and Jephthah, also of David and Samuel and the prophets: who through faith subdued kingdoms, worked righteousness, obtained promises, stopped the mouths of lions, quenched the violence of fire, escaped the edge of the sword, out of weakness were made strong, became valiant in battle, turned to flight the armies of the aliens. Women received their dead raised to life again. Others were tortured, not accepting deliverance, that they might obtain a better resurrection. Still others had trial of mockings and scourgings, yes, and of chains and imprisonment. They were stoned, they were sawn in two, were tempted, were slain with the sword. They wandered about in sheepskins and goatskins, being destitute, afflicted, tormented—of whom the world was not worthy. They wandered in deserts and mountains, in dens and caves of the earth. And all these, having obtained a good testimony through faith, did not receive the promise, God having provided something better for us, that they should not be made perfect apart from us (Hebrews 11:30-40).

INTRODUCTION

Faith in God can see us through any circumstance! Old Testament history marches forward with each generation supplying examples of faith. The verses studied in this chapter speak of Jew and Gentile, of male and female, and of the known and the unknowns of the faith.

The conclusion of chapter 11 records the valiant exploits and victorious endurance of faith. In all of Scripture, few passages are more inspiring than this. In the words of the writer of Hebrews, "time would fail me to tell" all that could be said about these heroes and heroines of faith.

This account does not simply list the miracles of faith, but it includes those whose faith cost them trials, misery and sometimes their lives. Whether faith brought deliverance or death, it is heralded in this great roll call of the faithful.

Faith in God helps us face the tough times of life. As faith encounters opposition and difficulty, it makes something out of those who live by it. This passage sets forth three wonderful results of faith during the tough times.

Faith Makes Conquerors out of the Obedient (11:30)

After 40 years of wilderness wanderings, Israel crossed the Jordan River miraculously. After this great triumph, they were faced with a large stronghold blocking their entrance into the Promised Land: the imposing city of Jericho. For the Promised Land to be claimed, this largest fortified city in Canaan had to be conquered. God told them to march around the city seven times and He would give them the victory. They obeyed and conquered.

When individuals come to know Christ and enter into their new life, immediately Satan may come against them with some seemingly impossible challenges. Any part of your life that is not surrendered to Jesus must be conquered before you can enjoy the fullness of life. Romans 8:37 says, "In all these things we are more than conquerors through Him who loved us." Obedience is the key to conquest.

Faith Makes Saints out of the Outcasts (11:31)

Rahab's life is a thrilling story. Rahab, a prostitute who plied her trade in the pagan city of Jericho, was a Gentile, coming from the people known as Ammonites. Joshua 2:9-11 records her confession of faith. "For the Lord your God, He is God in heaven above and on earth beneath" (v. 11). Her faith was based upon God's mighty acts.

When asking for mercy from the invading nation of Israel, she included her family in her request of protection. She obeyed instructions by tying a scarlet cord in her window (Joshua 2:18, 19). This was the sign of protection for her household. Rahab was saved physically, morally and spiritually.

The New Testament places three crowns on her head. Hebrews 11:31 crowns her for her *faith*. James 2:25 crowns her for her *fidelity*. Matthew 1:5 crowns her for her new *family*. And one of the most interesting things about Rahab is that she married a man named Salmon. Looking at the genealogy, we find she became the great-grandmother of David and an ancestor of Jesus Christ.

If God can save a pagan prostitute and put her in the line of Christ, is there any doubt that He can save you? Faith does not shut out the sinner—it is the sinner's last and best hope. Faith believes that God's great love seen in the death of Jesus, and His mighty power evidenced by the resurrection of Jesus, can save from sin. Anyone who by faith ties the scarlet cord of the blood of Jesus on his or her life is saved.

Faith Makes Heroes out of the Ordinary (11:32-40)

The clear truth revealed in these verses is that God uses ordinary people. Here we read of the unlikely and unknown living by faith.

The faith of the unlikely (11:32-35). The heroes found in the "Hall of Fame" are drawn from three periods of Hebrew history. Five are drawn from the period of the Judges. Gideon was fearful and hesitant, yet he became a mighty conqueror. Barak was also a hesitant leader, but he was inspired by Deborah to become a conqueror. Samson was weak and worldly, yet his faith wrought the victory at the end of his life. Jephthah was rash, yet he was faithful to his vow to God. Samuel, who was the last of the judges, was a great man of God, but he was careless with his own family.

These judges of Israel lived during a time when "everyone did what was right in his own eyes" (Judges 17:6; 21:25). However, these men rose above the dark age in which they lived to stand for God. None of these men were likely candidates for greatness, but God took them and used them in a mighty way.

David is the only hero mentioned from the Kingdom period of Israel. Here again we find an unlikely choice, but God chose this man to be Israel's greatest king. Even David's father, Jesse, did not see his potential since he did not include him in the lineup when Samuel came asking to see his sons to anoint one as king. God chooses the unexpected.

The third group mentioned in the "Hall of Fame" is the prophets, a group made up of different personalities. From the aristocrat Isaiah to the country farmer Amos, they were all God's choices. All of these saw great works wrought by faith.

Verses 33-35 speak of those who conquered kingdoms and claimed promises. Among them are Daniel, who shut the lion's mouth, and the three Hebrew children, who survived the fiery furnace. The key phrase is found in verse 34, "out of weakness were made strong." This is the secret of their conquering power. First Corinthians 1:27 says, "But God has chosen the foolish things of the world to put to shame the wise, and God has chosen the weak things of the world to put to shame the things which are mighty." It is not human strength or even strong faith that conquers. It is our faith in a strong God that makes the difference.

The faith of the unknown (11:35-40). Sometimes faith does not lead to immediate deliverance or release. This group is called simply "and others." Look at what they faced: mocking, scourging, imprisonment, stoning, torture, death, poverty and affliction. Furthermore, they were homeless wanderers. What does Scripture say of them? Verse 39 says they gained approval through their faith.

How we need to learn this lest we get out of balance in our beliefs! Faith in Jesus does not guarantee wealth, fame, healing or the easy life. Faith follows God obediently wherever He leads. Sometimes He leads through a difficulty. Sometimes He leaves us in a difficulty.

How can we answer the question "Why?" What can be said when someone who has lived for Jesus dies suddenly? What do we say when healing does not come? How do we respond when tragedy strikes a child? We answer with the Word of God, "of whom the world was not worthy" (v. 38). God has put His approval on the faith of the unknown and the unnamed faithful of a thousand generations.

CONCLUSION

The writer of Hebrews turns to those living after the coming of Christ and challenges them with the Word. These heroes believed before the promise was fulfilled in Christ. They had but the shadow and lived by faith. What a shame it would be for us who have the substance to draw back! We live on the other side of Calvary and the empty tomb. Dare we do less than those who lived on the "before" side?

Faith can conquer the stronghold of sin in your life. Faith can sustain the believer through every trial. We dare not go back. We dare not hold back. We must go where faith in Christ leads!

22

Don't Lose Heart

Therefore we also, since we are surrounded by so great a cloud of witnesses, let us lay aside every weight, and the sin which so easily ensnares us, and let us run with endurance the race that is set before us, looking unto Jesus, the author and finisher of our faith, who for the joy that was set before Him endured the cross, despising the shame, and has sat down at the right hand of the throne of God. For consider Him who endured such hostility from sinners against Himself, lest you become weary and discouraged in your souls. You have not yet resisted to bloodshed, striving against sin. And you have forgotten the exhortation which speaks to you as to sons: "My son, do not despise the chastening of the Lord, nor be discouraged when you are rebuked by Him; for whom the Lord loves He chastens, and scourges every son whom He receives." If you endure chastening, God deals with you as with sons; for what son is there whom a father does not chasten? But if you are without chastening, of which all have become partakers, then you are illegitimate and not sons. Furthermore, we have had human fathers who corrected us, and we paid them respect. Shall we not much more readily be in subjection to the Father of spirits and live? For they indeed for a few days chastened us as seemed best to them, but He for our profit, that we may be partakers of His holiness. Now no chastening seems to be joyful for the present, but painful; nevertheless, afterward it yields the peaceable fruit of righteousness to those who have been trained by it. Therefore strengthen the hands which hang down, and the feeble knees, and make straight paths for your feet, so that what is lame may not be dislocated, but rather be healed. Pursue peace with all people, and holiness, without which no one will see the Lord: looking carefully lest anyone fall short of the grace of God; lest any root of bitterness springing up cause trouble, and by this many become defiled; lest there be any fornicator or pro-fane person like Esau, who for one morsel of food sold his birthright. For you know that afterward, when he wanted to inherit the blessing, he was rejected, for he found no place for repentance, though he sought it diligently with tears (Hebrews 12:1-17).

INTRODUCTION

After reviewing the great heroes and heroines of faith, the writer of Hebrews sets forth the supreme example of faith. The Lord Jesus Christ laid aside the prerogatives of deity and lived His earthly life as the Man of God. He lived by faith in the Father. When we observe how Jesus ran the race of life, it should encourage us to be faithful.

All the believers of all the ages who have gone before are in the grandstand of glory looking down on us. Standing at the finish line is our Lord Jesus

Christ. As they cheer, Jesus beckons us onward to the finish line. These are not just spectators who are encouraging us—they are fellow contenders who have run the race of life already.

Notice that we are told to "run." There are four postures for the believer in the New Testament. First, the believer sits in heavenly places: "But God, who is rich in mercy, because of His great love with which He loved us, even when we were dead in trespasses, made us alive together with Christ (by grace you have been saved), and raised us up together, and made us sit together in the heavenly places in Christ Jesus" (Ephesians 2:4-6). This word speaks of our security in life.

Second, the New Testament also speaks of our *walk*: "I, therefore, the prisoner of the Lord, beseech you to walk worthy of the calling with which you were called" (Ephesians 4:1). "Therefore be imitators of God as dear children" (5:1). This speaks of the purity in which the believer is to live. The word *walk* speaks of the manner in which we are to live.

A third posture is found in the word *stand* (Ephesians 6:11, 14). This word speaks of our warfare as Christians.

The word in Hebrews 12:1 gives us the fourth posture of believers. We are to *run*. This speaks of our work as believers. There are some things that require haste, speed and endurance.

A balanced church must have all four postures. There are some churches that specialize in the "sit" posture, emphasizing our power in Christ over Satan.

Some emphasize the "run" posture, working diligently in evangelism. However, a balanced church must do it all.

Furthermore, these postures emphasize stages of maturity. A baby learns to sit, then to walk, then to stand and finally to run. There are but a few who are willing to run. The reasons for not attaining this fourth position are many. Among them is the problem of losing heart and growing discouraged.

How can we run this race of life and finish the course set before us? First we must face it honestly and understand what is involved.

The Difficulties of the Race (12:1-4)

There are two difficulties mentioned in these verses.

Encumbrances. "Let us lay aside every weight" (v. 1). The word *weight* means "burdensome load." A good athlete must be in shape and lay aside all weights and extra clothing to run a successful race.

Encumbrances may not be sinful. Many times believers sacrifice the best for the good. Christians can be burdened with so much work for God that they never get around to doing God's work in God's way! They get so involved in community affairs that are good in themselves that they miss the best.

It is easy for us to spend all our time in business, social, community, and personal activities that are good, and forget the race. Our lives can become like that closet you don't dare open because it is filled with clutter. Some can't "run" the race for Christ because life is too cluttered with activity. Churches can be cluttered with meetings, programs and activities that are good, failing to stay on the racecourse for Jesus.

During the American Revolution, a British admiral fired all his ammunition at a flag flying over a fort. He subsequently lost a battle at sea because of his foolishness to use his ammunition before the proper time. Let us not spend all of our time and energy on good things and miss the best.

Entanglements. The Bible speaks clearly when it points out how easily we can sin. We must strive against sin and resist it with all our heart.

Jesus Christ looked to the joy of victory. He looked beyond the Cross to the crown. He looked beyond the pain to the souls who would be saved. When life's race gets difficult, we must "consider Him" (v. 3). He fought sin by shedding His own blood. We ought to hate sin enough that we would rather die than let it hinder us in our run for God. We are to run with endurance because He endured. No difficulty should sidetrack us. Let us look further and see another thing that can cause us to lose heart in the race.

The Discipline for the Race (12:5-13)

Any runner knows that the body must be disciplined if the race is to be run to its finish. The same is true regarding our spiritual race. Our heavenly Father requires a disciplined people. God helps us by chastening and correcting us so that we can better run the race. In verses 5 and 6, the writer of Hebrews quotes

Proverbs 3:11, 12 to underscore the truth that the Father's discipline is not to cause us weariness—it is written to encourage and strengthen us for the race. In Hebrews 12 we see that chastening can serve as many things:

- A mark of His love (v. 6)
- A sign of sonship (vv. 6-8)
- A warning to repent (v. 9)
- An encouragement to holiness (v. 10)
- A training for fruitfulness (v. 11)

The Dangers of the Race (12:14-17)

The writer points out some dangers that can cause a believer to lose heart. These two dangers are not *outward* like the difficulties of the race. They are not *downward* from the Father, who disciplines us. Rather they are *inward*, hidden dangers. These are dangers to the heart and soul of a person.

Already we have been told to "look unto Jesus" and "consider Him" the Son of God. Also we have been told to be subject to the "Father of spirits" (v. 9). Now the sanctification of the Spirit in the inner man is brought into view. We must be clean on the inside, lest we fail to finish the great purpose of God for our lives.

The first danger is called "root of bitterness" (v. 15). This is the bad attitude toward others that poisons all of life. A root of bitterness comes when you refuse to forgive. It is another name for carrying a grudge or an ill will toward another.

A second danger is inward wickedness. Esau sold his birthright for a bowl of stew. He gave away the spiritual for the temporal. What he lost was irretrievable. Once given to another, the blessing could never be recalled.

This passage tells us three things sin will do to us. It can *entangle* you (v. 1). It can *cripple* you spiritually (vv. 12, 13). But worst of all, it can *stop* you (vv. 15-17). You can be less than the grace of God intended you to be. You can fall short of the finish line of your life. You can miss your potential. Esau did not lose his salvation, but he lost his blessing. The worst thing about giving an account to God will be seeing what we have done in comparison to what we could have done.

CONCLUSION

We have been given grace for the race ahead. Let us not stop until we cross the finish line. As we run the race, we can hear Abel cry, "Nothing but the blood." Enoch cries out, "Heaven is but a step away!" Noah cries out, "No disaster can stop you." Abraham shouts, "Remember, nothing is impossible." Sarah laughs and cheers, "You're never too old with God." Moses lifts his rod and shouts, "There is no foe that can stop you, and no sea that can drown you. Keep running." Rahab, whose face once bore the scars of sin, lifts up her voice and says, "There is no sin so great He can't cleanse, nor a life so broken He can't put back together."

Standing at the finish line is the One who stretches out a nail-pierced hand that once was nailed to a cross. He cries to us, "Follow Me. Run the race, run the race."

23

The Warning From Heaven

For you have not come to the mountain that may be touched and that burned with fire, and to blackness and darkness and tempest, and the sound of a trumpet and the voice of words, so that those who heard it begged that the word should not be spoken to them anymore. (For they could not endure what was commanded: "And if so much as a beast touches the mountain, it shall be stoned or shot with an arrow." And so terrifying was the sight that Moses said, "I am exceedingly afraid and trembling.") But you have come to Mount Zion and to the city of the living God, the heavenly Jerusalem, to an innumerable company of angels, to the general assembly and church of the firstborn who are registered in heaven, to God the Judge of all, to the spirits of just men made perfect, to Jesus the Mediator of the new covenant, and to the blood of sprinkling that speaks better things than that of Abel. See that you do not refuse Him who speaks. For if they did not escape who refused Him who spoke on earth, much more shall we not escape if we turn away from Him who speaks from heaven, whose voice then shook the earth; but now He has promised, saying, "Yet once more I shake not only the earth, but also heaven." Now this, "Yet once more," indicates the removal of those things that are being shaken, as of things that are made, that the things which cannot be shaken may remain. Therefore, since we are receiving a kingdom which cannot be shaken, let us have grace, by which we may serve God acceptably with reverence and godly fear. For our God is a consuming fire (Hebrews 12:18-29).

INTRODUCTION

In Hebrews 12, three truths encourage believers to be faithful in their Christian lives. First, verses 1-4 set forth the *encouragement of the race.* All of the faithful throughout history have endured the racecourse of life. Our Lord Jesus Christ has run the race as never before. Second, we have the *encouragement of the rod* (vv. 5-17). God will not allow the sin that entangles and cripples the faith life to go unanswered. He chastens His own. Finally, the Scripture text before us sets forth the *encouragement of the reward* (vv. 18-29).

Throughout the Book of Hebrews, the inspired writer has set forth the superiority of Christianity to the old covenant. The word *better* is used many times to declare what the believer has in Christ. Christ is *better* than the angelic hosts, *better* than Moses, serves as a *better* priest, has offered a *better* sacrifice, and has instituted a *better* covenant through the offering of *better* blood. All of this leads to a better life on earth because it is lived by faith. Furthermore, it leads to a better hope in the future because our reward is not earthly but heavenly.

Under the old covenant, the nation had come to Mount Sinai. Exodus 19:1-25 records those events. The Lord was on the mountain that burned with fire and was shrouded in a cloud. No one but Moses could approach the mountain—there God gave him the Law. What the people received at Mount Sinai revealed their lost and sinful state, but it could not save. It could regulate earthly life, but it offered no promise of eternal life. It could reflect one's spiritual condition, but it could never restore one's soul. Romans 8:3 says, "What the law could not do in that it was weak through the flesh, God did by sending His own Son in the likeness of sinful flesh, on account of sin: He condemned sin in the flesh."

Hebrews 12:18-21 gives us the joyous truth that Mount Sinai is not our home! Our future home is called Mount Zion. This is not a reference to our earthly Mount Zion in Jerusalem, but to the heavenly Jerusalem. Notice several truths about our superior residence in heaven.

The Description of Heaven (12:22)

Note the three descriptive terms used for heaven in this verse.

Mt. Zion. The word *Zion* literally means "fortress." This means a place of protection. Heaven will be a place where fear will be banished forever. The believer will live in complete security.

This is also the name of one of the chief mountains of Jerusalem. It was on Mount Zion that the Temple stood. Isaiah 8:18 declares that the Lord chose Mount Zion as His dwelling place. The people of Israel are called the daughters of Zion (2 Kings 19:21). Psalm 125:1 says, "Those who trust in the Lord are like Mount Zion, which cannot be moved, but abides forever." Zion represents the eternal Kingdom. Psalm 48:1-3 speaks of the redeemed in heaven as standing on Mount Zion: "Great is the Lord, and greatly to be praised in the city of our God, in His holy mountain. Beautiful in elevation, the joy of the whole earth, is Mount Zion on the sides of the north, the city of the great King. God is in her palaces; He is known as her refuge."

City of the Living God. God's heaven is described as a city. It was for this heavenly city that Abraham sought (Hebrews 11:10). It was for this city that the faithful of the Old Testament searched (11:13-16). It is this heavenly Jerusalem that God has prepared for all who love Him (11:16).

Heavenly Jerusalem. This description identifies that city with the New Jerusalem spoken of in Revelation 21:10-17:

And he carried me away in the Spirit to a great and high mountain, and showed me the great city, the holy Jerusalem, descending out of heaven from God, having the glory of God. Her light was like a most precious stone, like a jasper stone, clear as crystal. Also she had a great and high wall with twelve gates, and twelve angels at the gates, and names written on them, which are the names of the twelve tribes of the children of Israel: three gates on the east, three gates on the north, three gates on the south, and three gates on the west. Now the wall of the city had twelve foundations, and on them were the names of the twelve apostles of the Lamb. And he who talked with me had a gold reed to measure the city, its gates, and its wall. The city is laid out as a square; its length is as great as its breadth. And he measured the city with the reed: twelve thousand furlongs. Its length, breadth, and height are equal. Then he measured its wall: one hundred and forty-four cubits, according to the measure of a man, that is, of an angel.

Here is a traveling city, a 1,500-mile cube, whose description defies human comprehension. The size of the city is awe-inspiring. If it were divided into 78,000 levels 100 feet high, each level would contain 2,250,000 square miles. If you allocated 2,000 square feet for every person living there, you would have room for 43 billion persons. Of course, since that many persons have not lived since the beginning of time, there is plenty of room in the New Jerusalem!

The Population of Heaven (12:22-24)

Who will live in the heavenly Jerusalem?

The angels of glory. You will meet these glorious beings who have guarded and guided the works of God on this planet. You will meet the angel that was assigned to minister to you when you were saved (Hebrews 1:14).

191

The *church of the firstborn written in heaven*. This describes those of us who live in the church age. Those of us who belong to Christ from Pentecost to the Rapture are called "the church of the firstborn." The whole church will be gathered together in that day.

"God the Judge of all" (v. 23). God our heavenly Father will be there with us in that city.

"The spirits of just men made perfect" (v. 23). This is a reference to the Old Testament saints who looked forward to the coming of Christ and believed unto righteousness and salvation. This list includes Enoch, Abraham, Noah, Moses, David and Elijah, as well as millions who are unnamed and unknown.

"And to Jesus" (v. 24). We shall also see Jesus in that day. What a glorious moment that will be.

"And to the blood" (v. 24). It is because of His blood that the saints of all the ages can stand before Him in that day. That precious blood speaks for us in heaven. The blood of Jesus is the basis of our eternal redemption and security. Abel's blood could cry for vengeance. Jesus' blood cries for our pardon.

The Invitation to Heaven (12:25-29)

Look at the two possibilities in regard to the invitation to heaven.

1. *You may refuse the invitation* (vv. 25-27). These verses are a solemn warning to listen to Jesus. Those who refused Moses' word on this earth did not escape. Those who refuse the voice of Jesus from heaven will not escape. Presently the voice of Jesus speaks of salvation and forgiveness. One day His voice will be a

voice that will bring judgment to those who reject Him. Will you foolishly reject Him for that which is destined for destruction?

2. *You may receive the invitation* (vv. 28, 29). Receiving Jesus' invitation places you in an unshakable eternal Kingdom that will stand when this old earth is gone.

Having received that invitation, we are to serve God faithfully, wholeheartedly and reverently.

CONCLUSION

To refuse the invitation of heaven is to face God in judgment. "For our God is a consuming fire" (Hebrews 12:29). The fires of hell await those who refuse the voice of love and grace. Don't refuse His call.

24

The Christian Love Life

Let brotherly love continue. Do not forget to entertain strangers, for by so doing some have unwittingly entertained angels. Remember the prisoners as if chained with them—those who are mistreated—since you yourselves are in the body also. Marriage is honorable among all, and the bed undefiled; but fornicators and adulterers God will judge. Let your conduct be without covetousness; be content with such things as you have. For He Himself has said, "I will never leave you nor forsake you." So we may boldly say: "The Lord is my helper; I will not fear. What can man do to me?" (Hebrews 13:1-6).

INTRODUCTION

Having given us a glimpse of glory, the inspired writer brings us down to earth with some clear instruction on how we are to live. Looking in a Greek New Testament, you'd find the word *philia* used three times in this passage. This is a Greek word meaning "affectionate love." It is used in verse 1 as "brotherly love" (*philadelphia*). In verse 2 it is translated "entertain strangers," or "love guests" (*philoxenia*). It is found again in verse 5, translated "without covetousness," or "without love of money" (*aphilargyros*).

These verses speak boldly to us concerning several relationships of life. When we love the right things in the right way, our lives are deeper and fuller. The wrong kinds of love will enslave. Many live today under the tyranny of wrong love.

One may ask, "How can you know where to give your deepest affection?" It is simple. Just love the things Jesus loved.

My wife has a few keepsakes that belonged to her grandmother. Financially, they are not worth anything, but she loves them because her grandmother loved them. We ought to love the things Jesus loved.

Love Gives Vitality to the Church (13:1)

The word *philadelphia* has to do with Christian love toward one another. This word involves the practical expression of love. Those receiving the letter of Hebrews had this love already. In Hebrews 6:10 we read, "For God is not unjust to forget your work and labor of love which you have shown toward His name, in that you have ministered to the saints, and do minister." This church honored the name of Jesus by loving and caring for each other. They are exhorted to continue in that love for each other.

I once read a fictional account of a spaceship coming to the earth and taking a group of people captive. The aliens placed the people around a large table and tied one hand behind each one's back. The food was in the center of the table and each person was chained to his chair. Each was given a large spoon with which to eat. The spoons were long enough to get the food, but too long to get the food back to their mouths. They would have all starved unless one had realized that they could feed each other. We Christians need to assume our responsibility to care for one another seriously.

Love Displays Hospitality to the Stranger (13:2)

As believers, we are to show hospitality and love to those we may not know. This word could refer to both strangers who are lost and those who are saved. We never know who God may lead to our door or across our path.

In Genesis 18 we read the account of Abraham on the plains of Mamre. Little did Abraham know that the visitors he was receiving were heavenly guests. He entertained angels unawares. Manoah and his wife entertained "the angel of the Lord," according to Judges 13:15.

Christians are under a divine mandate to be friendly and hospitable. By opening our homes and our hearts, we can share a genuine witness with others. In addition, anytime fellow believers come to your house, they may be accompanied by "ministering spirits" (Hebrews 1:14).

In ancient times hospitality was a necessity because of the lack of hotels and the danger of robbers on the highway. Though every city has facilities today, our homes should be open to those who need a place to stay.

Home ministry is becoming the approach to witnessing and spiritual growth. Home cell groups are becoming the center of outreach and discipleship.

Love Demonstrates Sensitivity to the Hurting (13:3)

We need to be sensitive to the needs of those who are hurting. This verse mentions those in prison and those who may be ill-treated. Imprisonment was common in the persecution of first-century Christians.

In Hebrews 10:34 we find that this group had shown sympathy to the prisoners. Paul was imprisoned on at least three occasions. John was imprisoned on the isle of Patmos. Across the centuries, thousands of believers have known the deprivation of the dungeon. John Bunyan wrote the classic *Pilgrim's Progress* while in jail.

In our day, there are thousands of people imprisoned because of religious activities. Around the world, believers are being persecuted for their faith. This passage reminds us that they are a part of the body of Christ. We are one with them. The larger truth is that many of our fellow believers in America are prisoners. Some are prisoners of age, isolated in nursing homes. Some are prisoners of disease. Some are prisoners of difficult circumstances. Whatever the cause of enslavement, our love must show compassion to the hurting.

Christian Love Brings Sanctity to the Marriage Vow (13:4)

Today's society says marriage is outdated and parades a promiscuous lifestyle as normal. What the world calls a "swinger," God calls a *whoremonger*. What the world calls an "affair," God calls *adultery*. Marriage is to be held in honor (v. 4).

One of the church's biggest jobs is to strengthen marriages. Many churches have built *family life* centers. That is wishful thinking. Though recreational buildings offer a valid ministry, often these activities divide rather than unite the family. Only the home can be a family life center. The church must give the family time to be together.

We are to honor marriage and the home. Christians who are married are to keep their vows to one another. The church is to contribute to the strength of those marriages.

Christian Love Gives True Prosperity to the Individual (13:5, 6)

The writer says that our life is not to be characterized by the love of money. The Bible teaches that true prosperity is not found in material wealth. Jesus said, "For one's life does not consist in the abundance of the things he possesses" (Luke 12:15).

What does characterize true prosperity? The word *content* describes true prosperity. If we are content · with what we have, then the spirit of covetousness is broken.

First Timothy 6:6-10 speaks of true prosperity. "Godliness with contentment is great gain" (v. 6). Our treasure is the presence of God in our lives, and the peace and serenity we have on the inside. The rest of this passage in 1 Timothy warns us of the danger of worshiping wealth: "The love of money is a root of all evil" (v. 10).

The word *content* literally means "satisfied with sufficiency." Paul understood this when he said, "I have learned in whatever state I am, to be content" (Philippians 4:11). In 2 Corinthians 12:9, God says, "My grace is sufficient for you." When Paul faced his "thorn in the flesh," he drew on the grace of God and was content. That verse literally says, "My grace is sufficient to give you contentment."

In the latter part of Hebrews 13:5, and in all of verse 6, three wonderful confessions can be drawn. The writer quotes Deuteronomy 31:6 and Psalm 118:6. Because we have Jesus we can boldly confess: I am not alone, I am not ashamed, and I am not afraid—"The Lord is my helper; and I will not fear. What can man do to me?" (Hebrews 13:6).

True wealth is freedom from the tyranny of possessions and man's opinions. True prosperity is having the Lord as your friend and helper.

CONCLUSION

Our responsibility is to share His love. Our church life, social life, home life and business life must be characterized by His love.

When Doug Meland went to Brazil for Wycliffe to work on translating the Bible, the Fulnio tribe called him "the white man." After he labored among them for many years, they changed his title to "brother." The change came because of the care he showed them. As the old song says, "They will know we are Christians by our love." Let His love show in your life.

25

How to Recognize a Spiritual Leader

Remember those who rule over you, who have spoken the word of God to you, whose faith follow, considering the outcome of their conduct. Jesus Christ is the same yesterday, today, and forever. Do not be carried about with various and strange doctrines. For it is good that the heart be established by grace, not with foods which have not profited those who have been occupied with them. We have an altar from which those who serve the tabernacle have no right to eat. For the bodies of those animals, whose blood is brought into the sanctuary by the high priest for sin, are burned outside the camp. Therefore Jesus also, that He might sanctify the people with His own blood, suffered outside the gate. Therefore let us go forth to Him, outside the camp, bearing His reproach. For here we have no continuing city, but we seek the one to come. Therefore by Him let us continually offer the sacrifice of praise to God, that is, the fruit of our lips, giving thanks to His name. But do not forget to do good and to share, for with such sacrifices God is well pleased. Obey those who rule over you, and be submissive, for they watch out for your souls, as those who must give account. Let them do so with joy and not with grief, for that would be unprofitable for you. . . . Greet all those who rule over you, and all the saints. Those from Italy greet you (Hebrews 13:7-17, 24).

INTRODUCTION

The final verses of Hebrews are centered around three statements about spiritual leaders. Verses 7, 17 and 24 refer to "those who rule over you." The Greek for *those who rule* could literally be translated "leading or guiding men." This seems to be referring to pastors.

Four instructions are given to believers on how to respond to leadership:

- Remember them (v. 7)—recall with fondness.

- Follow them (v. 7)—receive direction.

- Obey and submit to them (v. 17)—honor them.

- Salute them (v. 24)—show affection.

These words speak of the pastor as one who gives direction, provides protection and deserves affection. Problems arise in a church, not in the willingness of God's people to follow a pastor, but in knowing the kind of man to follow.

We live in a day of cults, charlatans and wolves who come in sheep's clothing. In many cases, the blind are teaching the blind. This century has been inundated with the likes of Jim Jones and the Sun Myung Moon heresy. This is the day of high-handed liberalism that denies the basics of the faith, while drawing a salary from God's people. This is the day of distorted and compromised truth. How can anyone know the kind of leader to follow?

The Marks of a Spiritual Leader (v. 7)

There are three marks of a true spiritual leader.

Man of Truth. The first mark of a true spiritual leader is loyalty to the Word of God. Any person who has doubts about the truth of the Scripture has disqualified himself from spiritual leadership.

I have seen families who would seek a church on the basis of everything but the church's message. There is nothing wrong with looking at the ministries of a church to see if your gifts will fit. However, programs and ministries should be a secondary consideration to the message coming from the pulpit week in and week out. How tragic for a family to put their children under a dead or liberal ministry because of attractions only to buildings, programs, musical styles or tradition.

The true man of God will not check the wind to see which way it is blowing. He will preach the Word of God in love, no matter whom it affects. In the days of the great evangelist Billy Sunday, a woman criticized him for his hard preaching. "You are rubbing the fur on the cat the wrong way." Sunday replied, "The old cat's headed for hell. If it would turn around, I'd be rubbing it in the right direction!"

Man of Trust. The Scripture declares that the church is to follow a leader who leads by faith. The spiritual leader must be following Jesus so the people can follow Him. The word *follow* means literally "to imitate." They saw that a church eventually will take on the spirit of the pastor.

205

Man With a Clean Testimony. The phrase "considering the outcome of their conduct" (v. 7) literally translates "the goal of their lifestyle." Where does their conduct seem to be leading them? How do they live? Many who are in prominent positions of leadership live lives that are inconsistent with their message.

The Message of a Spiritual Leader (vv. 8-14)

The message of the true man of God will be centered on Jesus Christ. Three truths about Jesus Christ should undergird every message a pastor presents.

The Preeminence of Christ (v. 8). The unchanging Christ is the bedrock of the true spiritual leader. This message is unaffected by "various and strange doctrines" (v. 9). No, liberalism will not be a part of the message of the man of God. Recently a pastor said that we must change with the times. This was his excuse for taking an unbiblical stand. While our methods of presentation may change, Jesus Christ and His word are unchanging.

Christ is preeminent over legalism. To preach Christ is to preach grace, not the rules of religion. Christ is also preeminent over ritual. Verses 10 and 11 declare that the altars of the Old Testament were not sufficient to take away our sins. Religious ritual cannot save, only the unchanging Christ can.

The Passion of Christ (vv. 12, 13). Here the two words *suffer* and *blood* stand out. Our Lord suffered outside the gates of Jerusalem. He also suffered alone outside the fellowship of Israel and was cut off from the favor of heaven.

Our Lord Jesus went outside the gates of glory to come to this earth. He went outside the rights of His royalty and became a slave for us. He went outside the city of Jerusalem and wept and prayed in blood-shedding agony for our souls. Then the cursing crowd took Him outside the city to crucify Him, torture Him by the whistling lash, the cruel crown and the cross of crucifixion. He went as far as He could go to buy back our souls. He suffered for our sins. That is our message. We are to call men to leave all and follow Him. We are to be marked by His cross forever.

The Promise of Christ (v. 14). Our message should never lead anyone to be comfortable in this world. Our Savior who is alive is preparing a city for us, and one day will come to take us home. We should seek those things that are above. This should be the message of the man of God.

The Measure of a Spiritual Leader (vv. 15, 16)

The measure of a spiritual leader is not in numbers, buildings or human achievement. Though these things may be present, the proof of a true ministry will be in the people who are the product of that ministry. These verses indicate the three sacrifices God's people must offer.

Sacrifice of Worship (v. 15). Verse 15 indicates the importance of praise. Praise and thanksgiving are the hallmark of the worship of a people who are in love with Christ and led by His Spirit.

Sacrifice of Discipleship (v. 16). "Doing good" is a simple phrase that describes true ministry. God's people led wisely will do good morally, socially and spiritually. They will reach out to others to touch them in ministry.

Sacrifice of Stewardship. The word *communicate* (v. 16, KJV) is translated often as "share." People led rightly will give of their finances for God's glory.

CONCLUSION

Verse 17 declares that a pastor must be accountable to God as the guardian over the members in his church. Your pastor literally watches over your soul. He is to do it regardless of whether you receive instruction or reject instruction.

How do you relate to spiritual leadership? Do you remember to pray for your leader? Do you obey the Lord as the pastor shares His Word? No man of God can lead unless those under him will be led. No man of God can feed unless there are those who will be fed. You are the measure of your pastor's ministry. Your response will determine God's blessing on the church.

26

A Pastor's Heart

Pray for us; for we are confident that we have a good conscience, in all things desiring to live honorably. But I especially urge you to do this, that I may be restored to you the sooner. Now may the God of peace who brought up our Lord Jesus from the dead, that great Shepherd of the sheep, through the blood of the everlasting covenant, make you complete in every good work to do His will, working in you what is well pleasing in His sight, through Jesus Christ, to whom be glory forever and ever. Amen. And I appeal to you, brethren, bear with the word of exhortation, for I have written to you in few words. Know that our brother Timothy has been set free, with whom I shall see you if he comes shortly. Greet all those who rule over you, and all the saints. Those from Italy greet you. Grace be with you all. Amen (Hebrews 13:18-25).

INTRODUCTION

This message brings to an end our journey through the Book of Hebrews. These final words pull away the veil that hides the heart of the writer. Indeed, we discover the deepest desires and longings in the heart of the man of God.

Back in verse 17, the pastor is shown to be watchman over the people. As a watchman, he looks after the needs of the people. If it were possible to look into the heart of a true pastor, what would you see? There are three thoughts among many I believe you would observe.

A Pastor's Dependence on the People (vv. 18, 19)

The first phrase in this passage, "Pray for us" (v. 18), is most revealing. The writer, who I believe to be Paul, confesses his own need. Throughout his epistles, the great apostle pleads for the prayers of the people. "Pray at all seasons . . . on my behalf" (see Ephesians 6:18, 19). "Brethren, pray for us" (2 Thessalonians 3:1). "Now I beg you, brethren . . . strive together with me in your prayers to God for me" (Romans 15:30). "You also [are] helping together in prayer for us" (2 Corinthians 1:11).

A man of God certainly ought to have a prayer life. Beyond this he must have a lifeline of prayer support from the people he serves. The greatest need of a pastor is for a praying people. The request in Paul's prayer was for a clean life. Your pastor needs the protection of your prayers.

The Pastor's Desire for His People (vv. 20, 21)

The true pastor wants to see the deepest needs of his people met. Their needs can only be met as they know the Lord. After requesting prayer, the writer offers a prayer for the people. The content of this prayer touches their deepest needs.

It answers the problem of hostility. This prayer is offered to the "God of peace" (v. 20). The phrase is evidence to me that Paul wrote the Book of Hebrews. He is the only writer to use this exact expression in the New Testament. Six times Paul uses this phrase to answer the hostility and conflict people face.

Romans 15:33; 1 Corinthians 14:33; 2 Corinthians 13:11; and Philippians 4:9 all deal with God, who gives peace to the church. First Thessalonians 5:23 speaks of inner peace. "May the God of peace Himself sanctify you completely; and may your whole spirit, soul, and body be preserved blameless." This passage speaks to the conflicts that rage in the individual. Romans 16:20 declares, "The God of peace will crush Satan under your feet shortly." This declares that God has wrought the victory and given us peace in the victory of Christ over our Enemy, Satan. God is the answer to our hostility.

It answers the problem of mortality. The next phrase says, "Who brought up our Lord Jesus from the dead" (v. 20). We no longer have to fear death because Jesus conquered that enemy for us. When John Wesley's godly mother, Susanna, lay dying, her last request was, "Children, as soon as I am released, sing a psalm of praise to God." Her fear of death was broken by Jesus. Jesus destroyed the devil and the power of death, "and release[d] those who through fear of death were all their lifetime subject to bondage" (Hebrews 2:15).

It answers the problem of anxiety. The Lord Jesus is next called "the great Shepherd of the sheep" (13:20), because He is our true Pastor. In John 10:11, Jesus is called the "good shepherd" who dies for His sheep. In 1 Peter 5:4, He is described as the "Chief Shepherd" who is returning to reward His sheep. Here, in the text, He is described as the "great Shepherd" who watches daily over the lives of His sheep.

Psalm 23 reflects the attitude every sheep ought to have because of our Great Shepherd. The psalmist confessed "I shall not want" (v. 1) and also implied "I shall not worry." He could lie down in "green pastures" and walk beside "still waters" (v. 2). The soul was not weary—it was restored and healed.

If He is your Shepherd, you don't have to live with anxiety. Dr. Vance Havner once said, "Worry, like a rocking chair, will give you something to do, but it won't get you anywhere." Let us trust our Great Shepherd.

It answers the problem of iniquity. The next phrase says, "through the blood of the everlasting covenant" (v. 20). God has taken care of our guilt eternally! We are in a blood covenant with Jesus (see Hebrews 9—10). So many people are in terrible condition because of guilt. Through Christ you can know freedom and be released from that bondage.

It answers the problem of inability. Verse 21 speaks of God's work in His people. The phrase translated "make you complete" comes from the same word used for mending a net in Matthew 4:21. It refers to restoring that which is broken. It also refers to equipping an army for battle.

What this means to God's people is vitally important. The true pastor desires his people to know that

God will restore and equip them to do everything He needs to have done. When we operate in His power, He is pleased and receives all the glory.

A loving pastor desires for his people to have their needs met as he leads them to know Christ in a deeper and fuller way.

In these verses, we feel the heartbeat and sense the personal touch of the true pastor. He desires for his people to hear and heed the exhortation, or encouragement, he shares. The pastor is alongside his people to encourage them and keep them moving. This same word, *exhortation* (Hebrews 13:22), is used of the Holy Spirit in the Gospel of John, and is translated there as "comforter."

The Pastor's Dedication to His People (vv. 22-25)

The spirit of encouragement and helpfulness is seen in the author's concern for and desire to see the Hebrew Christians. His final blessing is, "Grace be with you all" (v. 25). What a way to end this glorious book that has declared the grace of God in Jesus Christ as superior to the law and ritual of the old covenant!

Grace, like the theme of a great symphony, crescendos again and again in this book. It is "by the grace of God" (Hebrews 2:9) that Jesus tasted death for us. Jesus sits on the "throne of grace" (4:16) to hear our prayers. Those who refuse salvation insult "the Spirit of grace" (10:29). God's undeserved favor has been poured out on us. Let us live according to His gracious Word, work and way.

CONCLUSION

Do you face the five problems mentioned earlier: hostility, mortality, anxiety, iniquity or inability? The God of peace—the Great Shepherd our Lord Jesus—can provide for you, make you adequate and give you victory in every situation. Will you trust Him today?